THE BURNING BUSH SYNAGOGUE / ARMON ARCHITECTS

„הנה הסנה בוער באש
והסנה איננו אכל..
(שמות פרק ג' פסוק ב')

STRUCTURE AND PRAYER IN

COMPREHENSIVE HARMONY

MASTERPIECE
SERIES

THE BURNING BUSH SYNAGOGUE / ARMON ARCHITECTS

FOREWORD BY MAJOR GENERAL AHARON HALIVA | INTRODUCTION BY MAJOR GENERAL GERSHON HACOHEN
ESSAYS BY ELIEZER ARMON AND DAVID AMGADI | PROJECT DESCRIPTION BY ELIEZER ARMON
INTERVIEW BY VLADIMIR BELOGOLOVSKY | EPILOGUE BY BRIGADIER GENERAL GAL HIRSCH
PHOTOGRAPHY BY URIEL MESSA, SABADOSH BENJAMIN, ELIEZER ARMON AND OSCAR RIERA OJEDA

OSCAR RIERA OJEDA
PUBLISHERS

"This book is dedicated to my beloved parents Moshe and Miryam Armon RIP, my wife Ruti, my sons Assaf and Itay, and my grandchildren Yaara, Nur and Itamar."

Eliezer Armon

CONTENTS

FOREWORD

BY MAJOR GENERAL AHARON HALIVA

Bahad 1 base was a home to me. It was there that I underwent the transformation from being a soldier into an officer and commander in the Israel Defense Forces. It was there that I was bestowed an entire world of values: of Zionism, of love for the Nation and the Land, of dedication and commitment to mission. It was there that I learned the true meaning of companionship and responsibility. I was also a company commander in Bahad 1, and trained infantry officers there.

Twenty years after my arrival at the Israel Defense Forces' Officer's Academy, I returned as its commanding officer. I had the privilege to educate, train, and transform thousands of young soldiers into the effective backbone of the Israeli Army.

I acted from the belief that the Israel Defense Forces and the State of Israel must have an officer school of the highest caliber, one grounded in spirit and deeds, and as such to ensure that from out of that school would emerge officers worthy to fulfill the mission of defending the State of Israel and its residents.

In that context, I also had the privilege of taking an active role in bringing the new synagogue of Bahad 1 into being.

David Ben-Gurion, who served as both the first Prime Minister and the first Defense Minister of the State of Israel, believed that the military history of the Jewish people was rooted in the beginnings of Jewish peoplehood. To Ben-Gurion, the Bible was a deep source of inspiration. He held the belief that our existence is dependent on a combination of the power of fire (literal military "firepower") alongside power of spirit.

Bahad 1 is an officers' school for the Jewish Army. Out of the thousands of soldiers who pass through its gates, emerge the next generation of Israel Defense Forces officers, leaders who will bear the yoke of senior military command on their shoulders, and become significant figures for the Jewish people and the State of Israel.

To know our history as Jews has a great value in shaping our characters as officers in the Israel Defense Forces. In order to know where we are going, it is incumbent upon us to delve deeply into understanding our roots, to learn, and to grasp from where we have come. Our Zionist-Jewish heritage and identity is a central axis in shaping our characters as officers and commanders in the Israel Defense Forces.

A synagogue is a distinct Jewish symbol that connects us to our past. The synagogue of Bahad 1 is located at the highest point in the officers' school campus. The story from which the synagogue draws its inspiration is that of the burning bush in the Book of Exodus. In the presence of the burning bush, Moses is transformed from being a simple

AHARON HALIVA, a Major General in the Israel Armed Forces, was born in 1967 and joined the paratroopers brigade in 1986 where he served in several command positions. Currently he is the head of operations directorate of the Israel Defense Forces' general stuff. He is a graduate of national security college, has a B.A. degree in social Sciences from Bar-Ilan University and a M.A. degree in social science from the political science school of Haifa University.

shepherd to the future leader of the Jewish nation who will lead them out of slavery to freedom.

On the parade ground of Bahad 1, where in the background stands the synagogue surrounded by concrete flames, the young officers are given the mission and responsibility to lead and command Israeli soldiers, to transform from ordinary soldiers to officers in the service of the nation and State of Israel. From a military commander, and a civilian leader, the same qualities are required: the ability to motivate and move people, determination, compassion, good listening, patience, modesty, wisdom, resourcefulness, boldness and courage. The military commander, like the civilian leader, must serve as a paragon and symbol. This is also the point where fire power and spirit are joined together – past and future, history and vision, sword and scroll. The fire of the burning bush, the pillar of fire before the camp, the fire of battle.

I am not a religious person. I define myself as a culturally secular believer. Judaism, including the synagogue, is an essential part of my identity as an individual and an officer in the Israel Defense Forces. The IDF officer training course is demanding and long. Alongside physical and mental challenges, cadets engage in the study and clarification of values and norms, as well as the strengthening of their greater consciousness and identity.

I can recall many occasions as Commander of Bahad 1 where I met secular-traditional and religiously Orthodox cadets, both men and women, in the synagogue. I also was witness to occasions where the synagogue was full to capacity, such that many cadets had no choice but to stand outside in order to listen to the prayer service. Among them, some came for religious motives, and many others came to experience, to feel the excitement, and connect with the sources.

There is no more suitable place than the synagogue of the officer's training school of the Israel Defense Forces to read from the siddur – the traditional Jewish prayer book – and recite the blessing: "May He who makes peace on high, may He in his mercy make peace for us, and for all of his nation, Israel. And let us say: Amen."

Tel Aviv, Israel February 2020

INTRODUCTION

BY MAJOR GENERAL GERSHON HACOHEN

Sketch of Joshua's Altar on Mt. Ebal.

The Officer's Academy's Synagogue
"A Continuous Fire Will Burn Upon the Altar"

Under the lights of night, the synagogue in the Israel Defense Forces' Officer's Academy appears as a flame rising from the altar. The bottom floor, with the declining stairs right-angled to the building, is the altar; the sanctuary above is the fire elevating to the heavens. Prayers are held in the heart of the concrete flames that make up most of the building. From an external perspective of its proportions, the entire building emulates the temple's altar. According to the archaeologist Adam Zertal, the Yehoshua Ben Nun altar on Mount Aval has similar proportions.

Eliezer Armon, an architect, who designed and constructed the synagogue, honestly admits that the dimensions of an altar were far from his mind. When the planning began, he sought to design the building so it would embody the essence of Moses in front of the burning bush on Mount Sinai. Inspired by the symbolism of this event as an epic moment for the duty of leadership placed on the shoulders of Moses, and with clear and attentive distinction of terms, Eliezer Armon approached the planning attempting to engulf the synagogue in the flames of the never-consuming fire. There, facing the eternal flames, Moses answered God's call and said, "I am here."

What we have before us is a familiar phenomenon from the art world – the architect planned the structure with the expectation it would express the flames of the burning bush, but for me, at first glance, the building appears to be burning flames over the temple's altar. The renowned philosopher, Ludwig Wittgenstein, focused on this duality and described the term "seeing-as" (as in the Duck-Rabbit painting: one sees a duck, and another sees a rabbit). However, something much more significant is taking place, a deep bond is developing between the burning bush and the temple's altar. The altar on the temple's grounds, on which an eternal

GETERGERSHON HACOHEN, a retired Major-General in the Israel Defense Forces, is a senior research fellow at the Begin-Sadat Center for Strategic Studies and advisor to Our Soldiers Speak. He holds a B.A and M.A in philosophy and comparative literature from the Hebrew University of Jerusalem.

From 1973 to 2015, Gershon Hacohen was a member of the IDF (Israel Defense Forces). In the '73 war, he fought on the Sinai front and west of Suez Canal. He served on the Syrian front in 1974, participated in combat in Lebanon, the West Bank, and the Gaza Strip, and also served in all command levels in the Armored Corps, including the 7th Brigade. He commanded divisions 36 and 319, and commanded a division during the disengagement from Gaza in 2005. In 2006 he was appointed Major General, and in subsequent posts served as commander of the Israel Defense Forces' Military Colleges and commander of the Northern Corps.

flame burned, actually pointed to one of the temple's common rituals to institutionally commemorate the burning bush, following the commandment that "And a continuous fire must continue to burn upon the altar."

This verse was addressed by the "Admor HaZaken" Shneur Zalman of Liadi, as discussed by Dov Ber ben Avraham of Mezeritch (Maggid of Mezritch):

"In the Mishkan, the tabernacle, built by the Israelites in the desert, and in the temple, the children of Israel made sacrifices to God, and the fires would descend from the heavens and accept their offerings." Even though fire descended from above, which show an inner awakening and readiness for divine interaction, the beginning of this event was started by the children of Israel below. They would have been required to initially bring a simple source of fire so it could be used to build the fires so the awakening flames would flicker towards the heavens. And written in the Zohar: "the spirit of awakening generate the spirit and uplift it." In other words, the spirit of awakening amongst the children of Israel on earth uplifts the spirit and willingness to connect with the heavens. And this is one of the commandments in the Torah instructing us to "light a simple fire on the altar to awaken the fire of the heavens".

These passages hold the deep mystery of the human being's obligation to awaken and take action for their own redemption. This must begin with their own efforts in the material world as a condition for evoking salvation from above. This message defines the moment leadership was born – to remove oneself from among their brothers, and to take the initiative. This was the logic underpinning the roots of the Zionist revolution – recognizing the duty to awaken for practical action. In the *History of the War of Independence*, Ben-Gurion wrote: "We achieved victory in three paths: the path of belief and trust, the path of pioneering creativity, and the path of suffering." (*History of the War of Independence*, Introduction by David Ben Gurion, Ma'arachot Publishing,

The Burning Bush synagogue, view from northwest.

1959, p. 39). There is a direct connection between Moses undertaking the burden of leadership for the salvation of the children of Israel from Egypt, and for Israel's redemption in the modern era. They are connected by the willingness to undertake a path of suffering and sacrifice taken from the moment Moses passionately said, "Here I am."

The sages adhered to the principle of sacrifice that lies within "Here I am," and emphasized the special addition coined by Isaiah the Prophet, "Here I am. Send me". As it is written "I will hear God's voice asking 'Whom shall I send? And who will go for us?" and I said, "Here am I. Send me." (Isaiah 6:8). To emphasize the extent of the sacrifice of Isaiah's sacrifice for this undertaking, the Talmudic Midrash expands and explains: it was as if the lord was shouting at himself, "Whom will I send? Who will take this upon himself and be my messenger, I sent Micha and he was defeated, I sent Zachariah and he was killed, Jeremiah was cast into a cistern, and Isaiah responded: 'Here I am. Send me.'" (Piskata Rabbati, 33:19). These were the words used by our sages to express the idea that this undertaking, by its very nature, requires dedication and sacrifice, especially in life-threatening circumstances.

Upon entry into Canaan, Abraham built altars in Alon Moreh and in Beit El, as it is written "There he built an altar to the Lord and called on the name of the Lord." (Genesis 12:8). Compared to other altars that Abraham built, the most important one was built for the sacrifice of Isaac on Mount Moriah. As dramatically detailed: "When they reached the place God had told him about, Abraham built an altar there and arranged the wood on it. He bound his son Isaac and laid him on the altar, on top of the wood." (Genesis 22:9). There it was forever determined that human sacrifices will no longer be offered to God. With the calling of the angels from heaven: "Do not lay a hand on the boy," the emphasis is placed on the extent to which a person is willing to make such a sacrifice, and in this heroic moment, limits were placed on this level of compliance. The Torah was so adamant about the over-willingness towards human sacrifice, that it issued an echoing condition for the manner in which the altar was to be built: "And when you make for me an altar of stones, you shall not build them of hewn stones, lest you wield your sword upon it and desecrate it." (Exodus 20:22). In the archeological excavations carried out by Adam Zertal on Mount Ebal, an altar was discovered that was built by Yeshua Ben Nun, and it was indeed found to be constructed of natural stones that were never touched by iron tools. The sages expanded on the Torah's restriction for building the altar: "Since iron was created to shorten man's days and the altar was created to prolong man's days, and it is not right therefore that that which shortens should be lifted against that which prolongs." (Mishnah, Middot, Chapter 3). Rashi later comments that: "the altar makes peace between Israel and their Father in heaven. Therefore, the cutter and destroyer shall not come upon it." (Mekhilta, Middot). In the spirit of this reservation originating from human sacrifice, the value of unequivocal devotion towards the sanctity of human life is interwoven throughout the Bible. This is the message Hanna expresses when Shmuel the Prophet brought her to Eli the Priest in the Tabernacle in Shilo, "For this child did I pray, and the Lord granted me my request, which I asked of Him. And I also have lent him to the Lord; all the days which he will be alive, he is borrowed by the Lord." (Shmuel I, 1:26-27). From within their deep understanding of the message held in Hanna's story, the sages determined it be read at the highpoint of the Rosh Hashanna prayers, just prior to the sounding of the shofar. Therefore, there is a call for comparison between the story of the sacrifice of Isaac and the story of Hanna. Abraham and Isaac walked towards the altar, father and son, in complete sacrifice, as it is written, "and they walked together." Hannah and Shmuel walked towards the Tabernacle in Shilo, mother and son, with the same level of compliance, however Hannah hands her son to another, and certainly did not sacrifice him. She only "lent" him, to realize his life's destiny. And maybe, under the epos of a mother releasing her son for his calling, Ben-Gurion made his famous statement: "Let every Jewish mother know that she has entrusted the lives of her sons in the hands of commanders worthy of that trust." The wonder of sacrifice shown in the giving-away of her son for the Lord's service, together with the almost miracle of Moses' accepting his responsibility in front of the burning bush, intertwine with the synagogue in the Officer's Academy.

The synagogue towers over the parade grounds for every final ceremony, as if it were an altar, with its blazing flames and tradition of sacrifice, from the sacrifice of Isaac until today. Professor Yeshayahu Leibowitz, a disciple of 19th-century enlightenment, attempts to break the relationship between the story of Isaac's sacrifice and the readiness for continued sacrifice that continues to be vital in our struggles for survival. It is worthwhile to focus on his words to understand the message echoing in the synagogue constructed by Eliezer Armon. Leibowitz wrote:

Emancipation from the cables of slavery to nature is only achieved by religion and fulfilling commandments. And the overcoming of one's inclinations evolving from a philosophical school of thought or other secular traditions cannot achieve this. The truth is that the trend of secularization in all discourse of traditional values has also diminished from the term Isaac's sacrifice. Today, we leniently use this term to describe acts of heroism that lack any religious significance, such as parents who sacrifice their children – or in any case, came to terms with their death, in the wars of our independence and survival. This type of usage is a mistake: the patriarchs and matriarchs who suppressed their natural love and compassion, rejected human values for others, which they themselves recognized as having a higher value that justified all sacrifice – the nation and the homeland. This is in no way similar to Isaac's sacrifice, where without any incentive, all human values that can classified as human understanding and feeling were silenced – and rejected by God's glory and majesty." (Yeshayahu Leibowitz, Practical Deeds, from Machenayim).

Leibowitz's words express a modern and enlightened approach that completely separates religion and its values from other human phenomena considered in everyday practical reasoning. Leibowitz reduces the religious phenomena, removing it from the deliberations of today's world. The basis of this distinction is the Christian discernment between a kingdom in the heavens and a kingdom on earth. In contrast, Armon's synagogue, like the altar, expresses the hybrid connection between heaven and earth. Just like the fire over the altar flickering towards the heavens, which begins with mankind and its actions on earth and touches the heavens, the synagogue's presence in the heart of the Officer's Academy serves as a holistic connection that exists over areas that are seemingly separate. The words of Nehama Yisraeli, a Palmach soldier from Kibbutz Dovrat, who lost her two sons in armor battles along the Suez Canal in the Yom Kippur War (October 1973), illustrate this noble connection, that cannot be separated from either religious or human sacrifice. In one of the memorial services, she said, "a person who does not have a value he is willing to jeopardize his life for, or even sacrifice his life, then he has nothing of value to live for."

In the unique and special structure built by Eliezer Armon, in the form of an altar, with flames engulfing the sanctuary, a new idea was created – a place that is special. This distinct location not only expresses the unique connection between the heavens and the earth, but much more. It creates a unique connection between past and present Jewish tradition – from Abraham and Moses, to the young Israelis entering the Israel Defense Forces' Officer's Academy to undertake the tradition of service and dedication.

ESSAY

BY ELIEZER ARMON

Moses in front of the burning Bush.

The Burning Bush synagogue in BAHAD 1.

The Idea Behind the Building
The Spirit

"and although the bush was on fire, the bush was not consumed" (Exodus 3:2).

It was upon witnessing the burning bush that Moses received the role of leading the Jewish People. And like him, upon receiving the rank of an officer, soldiers undertake the role of military command and leadership while the bush is burning in their background, reminding them of Moses' commitment.

This was the inspiration behind the design of the building and its representation of the burning bush. The concrete flames engulf the officer in the fire of service during prayer. Fire is the main motif in the military experience. The raging flames have military and military unit insignias included in them. Fire is also a significant motif in the field of battle, and the basis of every military organization that operates according to defined "open fire" engagements.

The building is conspicuous, so it can be seen from the parade grounds and serve as a symbol to every cadet during their training, and as a background when the coveted officer's commission is awarded.

Architect Eliezer Armon together with Gabi Ashkenazi, IDF chief of staff at the time (above). After the destruction of the Israelite temple, the MENORAH is being carried by Jewish prisoners of war to Rome. A template from Titus' arch of triumph (below). View from the prayer platform (Bimah) to the Holy Ark (Aron Ha'kodesh) (following spread).

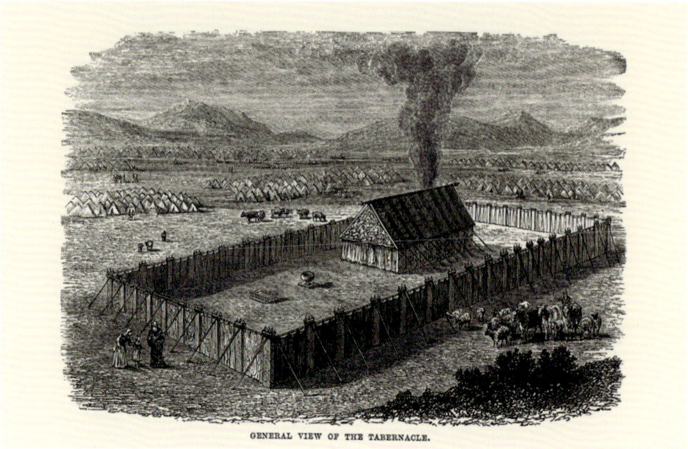

The vision of Jacob's ladder. Color lithograph by L. Gruner after N. Consoni after Raphael. Credit: Wellcome Collection (above). The ancient Israeli tabernacle – the MISHKAN. A sacrifice taking place in the tabernacle in the wilderness; the encampments of the Jewish tribes spread out to the horizon. Color lithograph. Credit: Wellcome Collection (above right).

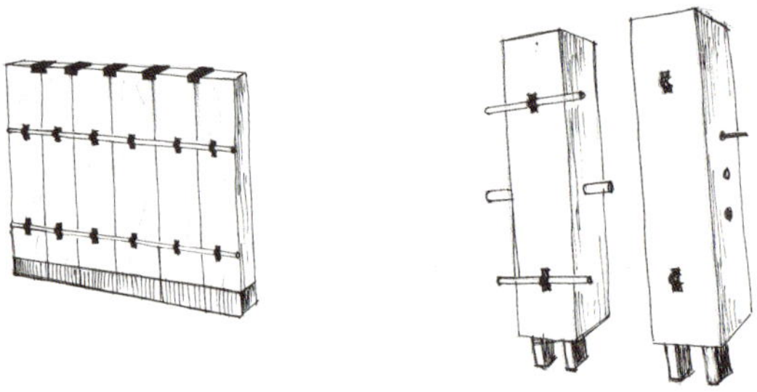

The Incline to the Prayer Hall

The synagogue is reached by traversing an incline. Each step distances us from the physical world and brings us closer to the spiritual. While planning the synagogue, we contemplated which materials were to be used to build its main entrance door. It only felt natural that the cadet who comes for prayers will arrive through a screen of fire. The sun setting in the west and copper has enabled us to create the feeling of a blazed door. We were able to connect the physical to the spiritual.

The Bridge

"The entire world is a very narrow bridge," said Rabbi Nachman of Braslev, and there, between the heavens and the earth, unstable, dependent on the compassion of our creator, we enter the gates of the prayer hall, full of spirit and belief. The synagogue has two entrances. The main one in front of the copper-clad door burns like a flame of fire as the sun strikes it. The second is a bridge suspended between heaven and earth following the Rabbi's statement.

The Flame

Each element of the flame is attached with two steel rods on the upper part, and two lower anchoring points, fastened with screws, on the lower part. Each group of three flames was anchored by means of a horizontal iron rod so the walls of the tabernacle will be stable. This was inspired by the design of the ancient Israeli tabernacle (MISHKAN), which according to the Bible, was built by the lord's commandment while in the Sinai desert. "The middle bar in the center of the boards shall pass through from end to end." (Exodus 26:28)

The Prayer Hall

The prayer hall is comprised of 24 prefabricated concrete flames, which are attached to a concrete frame and fastened with screws and steel rods produced in an industrialized and controlled process, with precision measured in millimeters. The synagogue's ceiling has been fitted with detached lighting elements that make up a seven-armed menorah, one of the temple's sacred tools of worship. There, with the cadet completely wrapped in flames, the menorah hovers above.

The back entry bridge at twilight. Photograph by Uriel Messa.

Installation of the concrete flames. Photograph by Eliezer Armon.

The Praying Stool

From the Book of Judges 7:5-8, the story of Gideon is told, when he chose the best of his warriors:

"So Gideon took the men down to the water. There the Lord told him, 'Separate those who lap the water with their tongues as a dog laps from those who kneel down to drink.' Three hundred of them drank from cupped hands, and all the rest got down on their knees to drink. The Lord said to Gideon, 'With the three hundred men that lapped I will save you.'"

Gideon chose to enter battle with soldiers who did not relinquish their weapons when drinking water. This story inspired me when I planned the praying stools. I suggested to the commander of the Officer's Academy at the time, Colonel Aharon Haliva, to link the "sword" – the soldier's weapon – to the prayer by means of a designated rack to hold their personal weapons during prayer so they will be able to pray with their weapons easily accessible. This is how a rack was created for the soldiers and cadets who pray there. The weapon rack serves as a legacy to Gideon and his tradition, that a soldier never leaves his weapon.

Development

We surrounded the site with olive trees, inspired by the officer's pin portraying an olive branch wrapped around a sword. This orchard of olive trees is interwoven with the flames of being called to service. This symbol is called "the platoon commander pin." It originates from the Palmach, the precursor of the Israel Defense Forces. In the the Palmach, commanders used to wear this pin on their shirts. The sword wrapped in olive leaves symbolize that even in times of war the purpose of the fighting forces is to bring peace. The olive leaves represent peace like the first olive leaf that was brought to Noah's Ark by the pigeon proving that the world is safe again to live in.

A prayer stand imitates a weapon's barrel as inspired by the story of Gideon in the book of Judges. Photograph by Eliezer Armon.

The IDF platoon commander's pin.

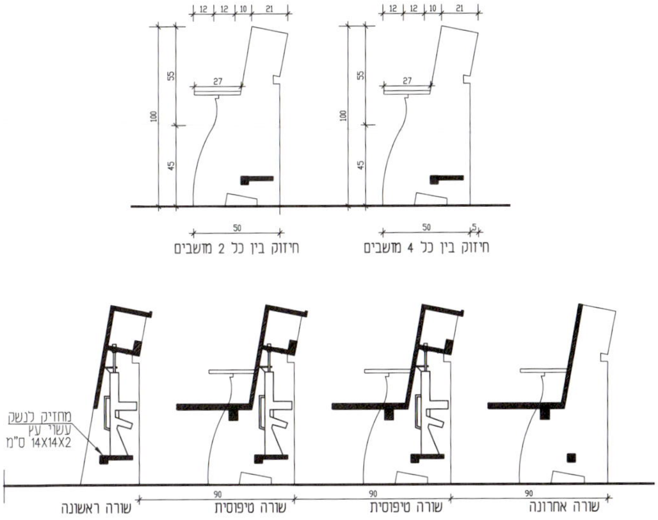

Working drawing of a prayer stand with a weapon's barrel.

DESIGN

DESCRIPTION

BY ELIEZER ARMON

A two-floor building made from exposed architectural concrete, reaching a height of 14 meters. The ground floor stretches over an area of 100 square meters. There is a classroom, an office for the base's rabbi, and all the necessary amenities. The floor above, the prayer hall, stretches over an area of 265 square meters. It contains a large open space, including the women's prayer section of 40 square meters. The base of the hall is a floor situated over the walls of the lower floor that juts out as a cantilever around the perimeter.

The synagogue is surrounded by 24 prefabricated wave-like flames, with a width of 180 cm, a thickness of 22 cm, and each being some 10 meters long. The prefab "concrete flame" that extends ever upwards, rests on the floor and is connected at a height of 7.5 meters to the synagogue ceiling, each by means of two steel elements.

The prefabricated elements are arranged in opposing positions, concave vs. convex. The geometrical structure allows natural light to enter through the openings created between them.

To enhance the building's stability, at key points between elements, a solid 25-cm-wide steel rod was inserted through a sleeve. Each sleeve connects three elements; epoxy grout was injected to connect the elements into one reinforced system.

The synagogue has three entrances: the main entrance level from the west; the south, which is equipped with a ramp to serve the disabled; and the southern entrance, which is also used to access the women's prayer section. The synagogue "overlooks" the parade grounds located on the southwestern edge of the Officer's Academy's base, next to the current synagogue that was designed by the renowned architect, Zvi Hecker.

An upper section of the curved concrete flames (opposite page).

SKETCHES

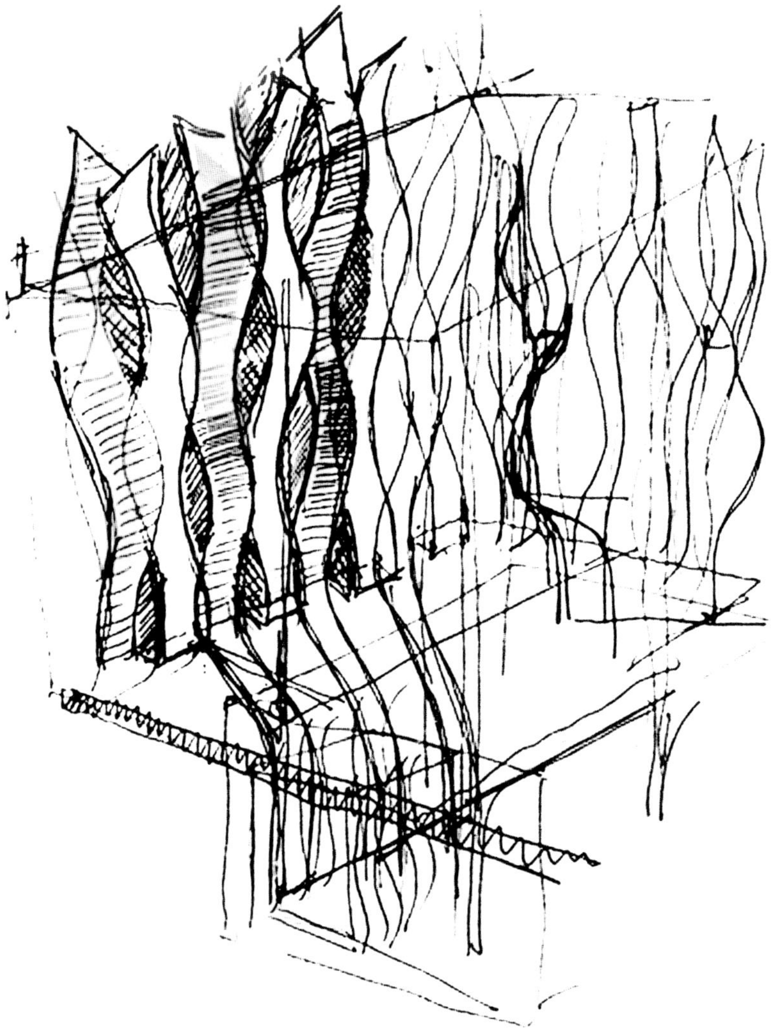

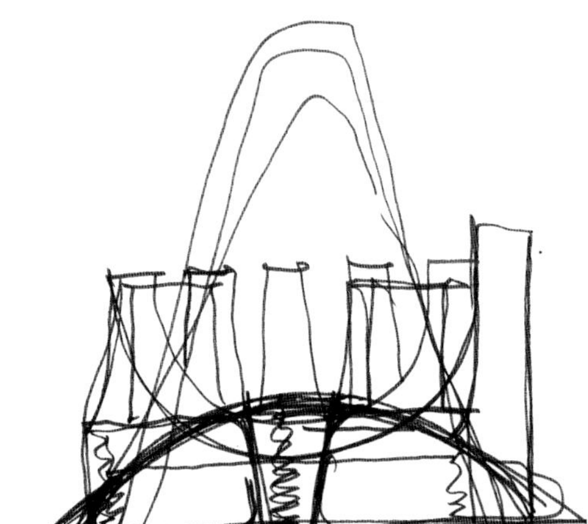

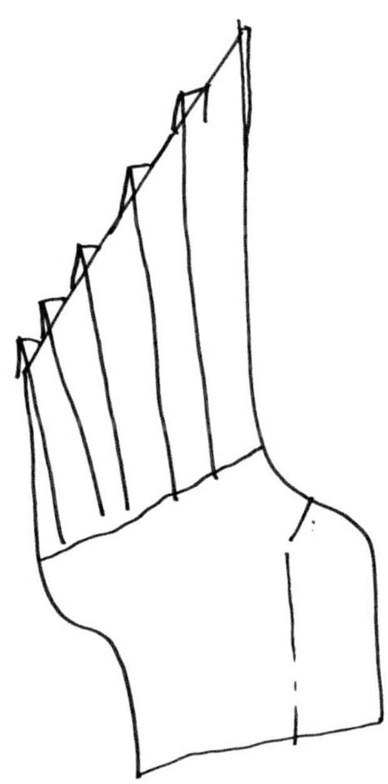

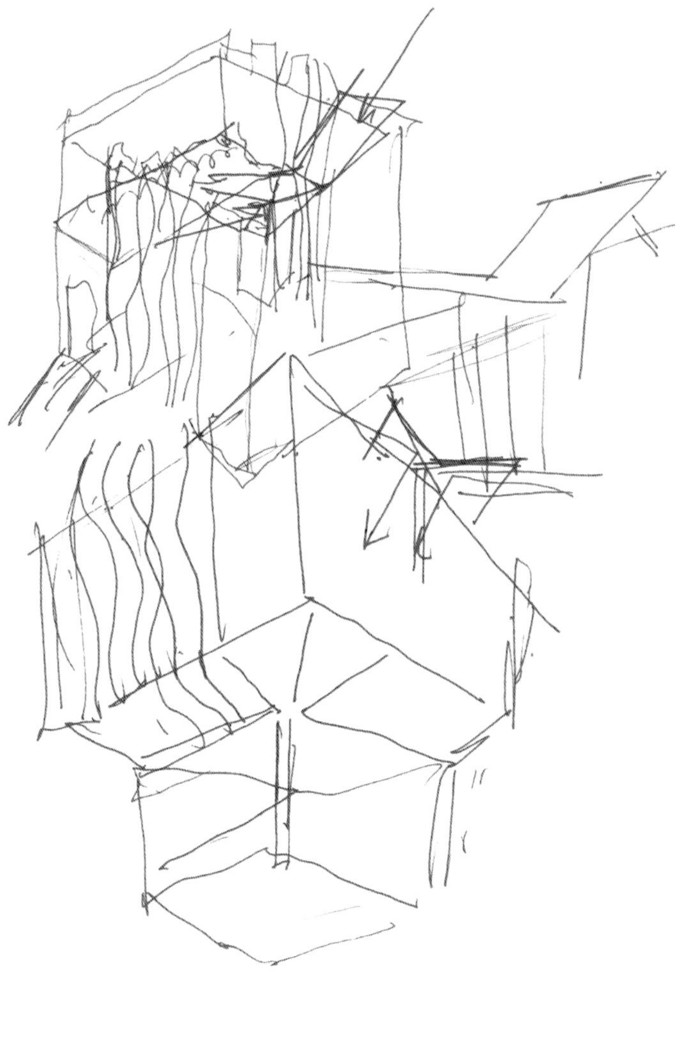

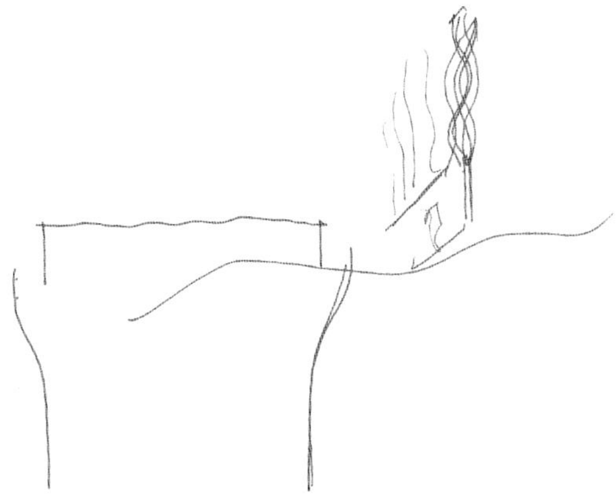

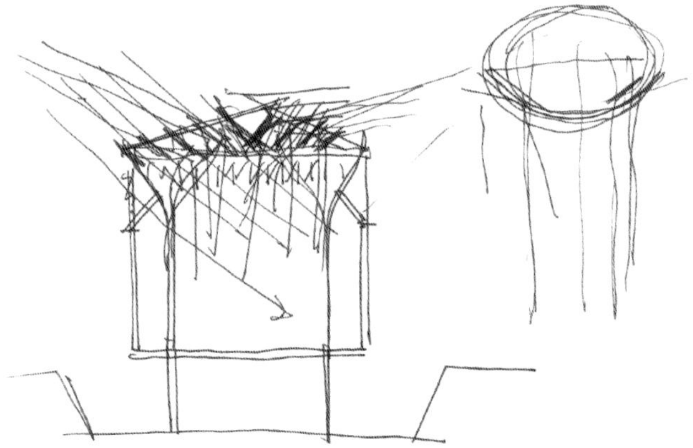

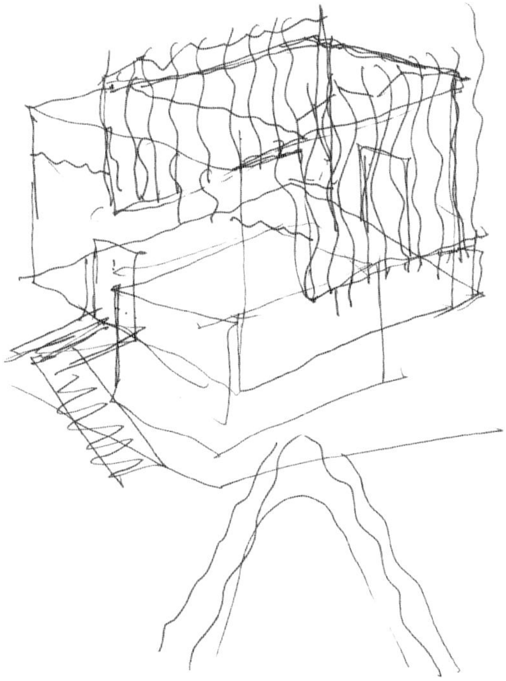

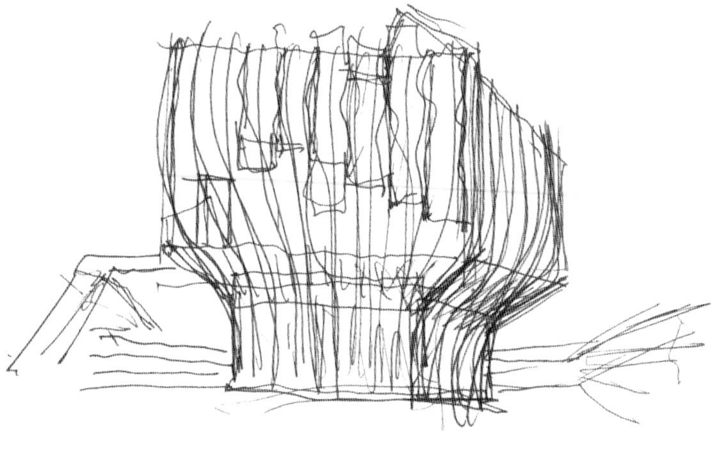

PRESENTATION DRAWINGS

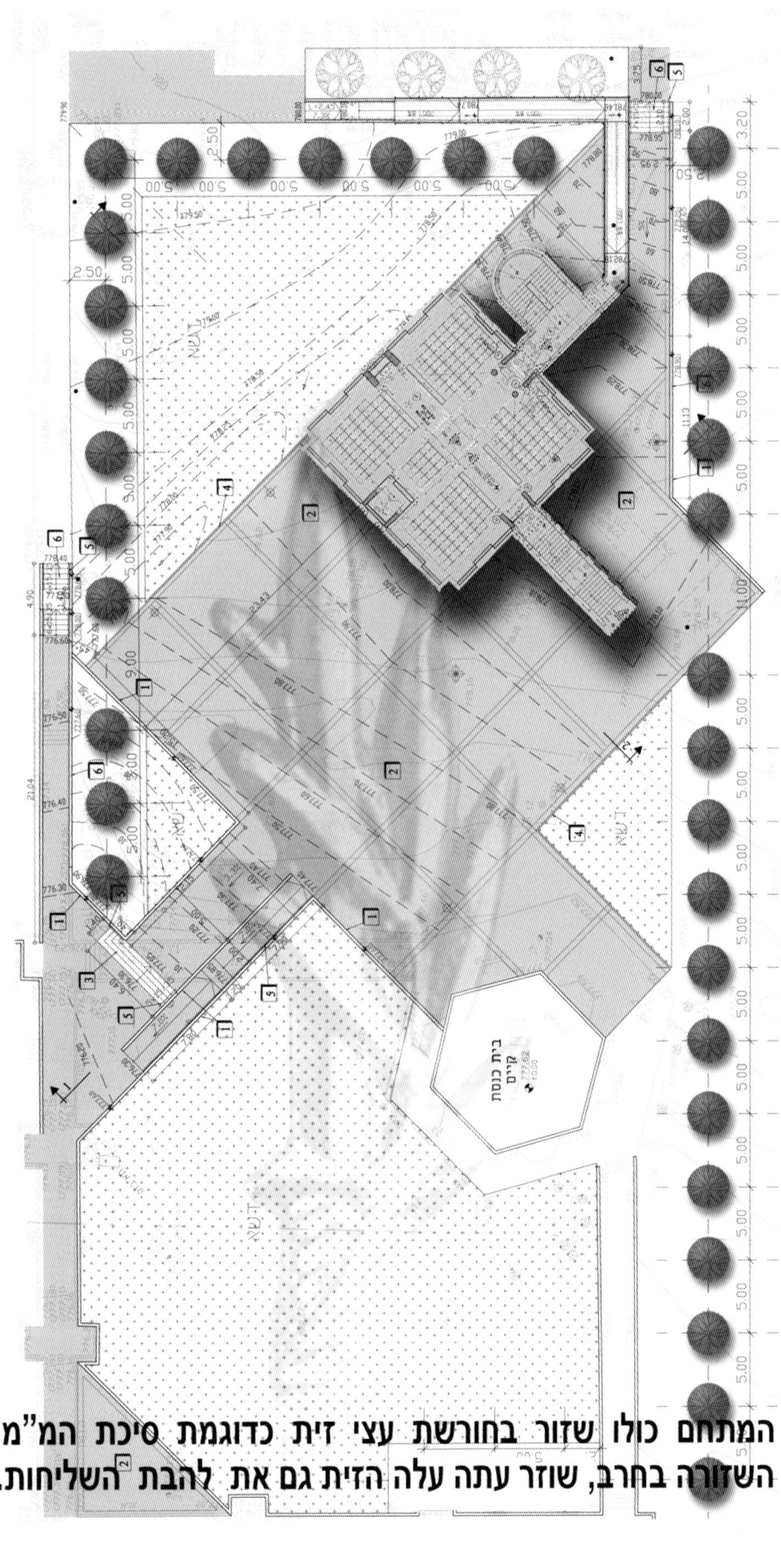

המתחם כולו שזור בחורשת עצי זית כדוגמת סיכת המ"מ השזורה בחרב, שוזר עתה עלה הזית גם את להבת השליחות.

The whole compound is interwoven with a forest of olive trees as the sword is interwoven in the officer pin, the olive branch now entwining the flame of appointment.

Site Plan

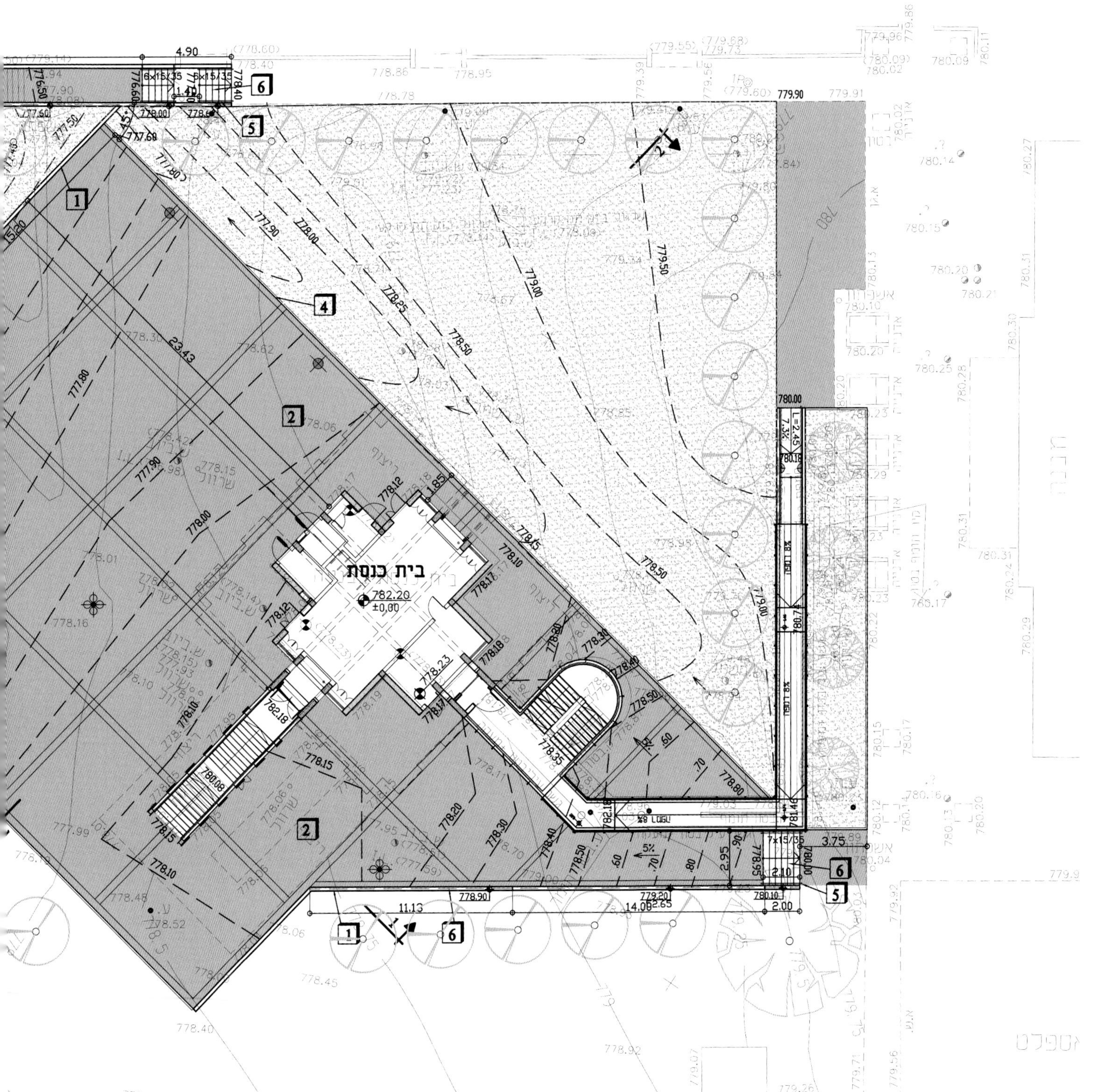

פיתוח כללית

קנ"מ: 1:250

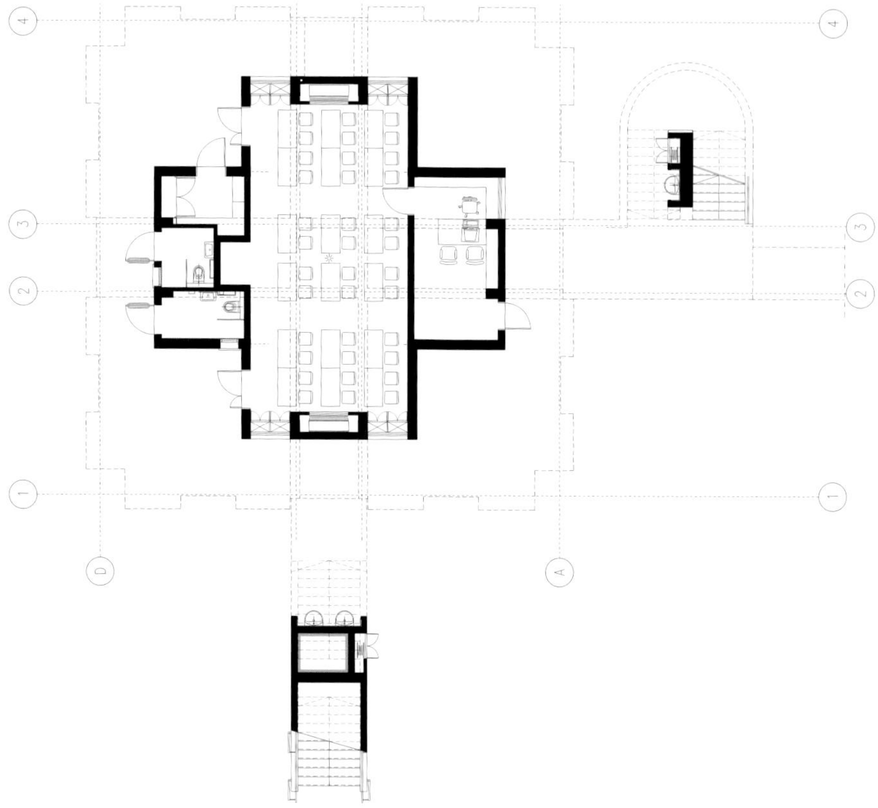

Entrance Floor

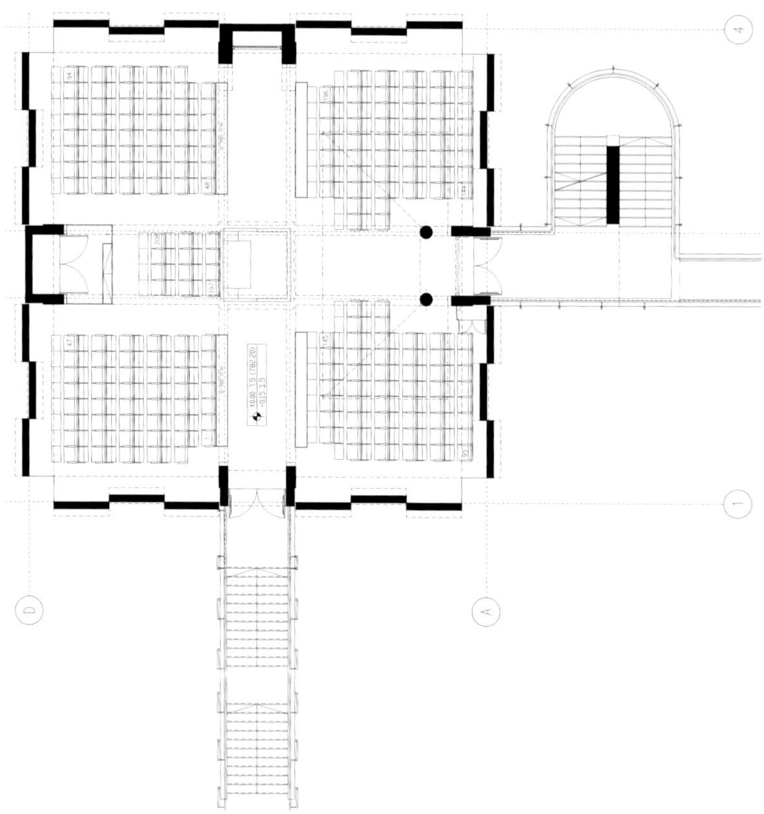

Main Floor

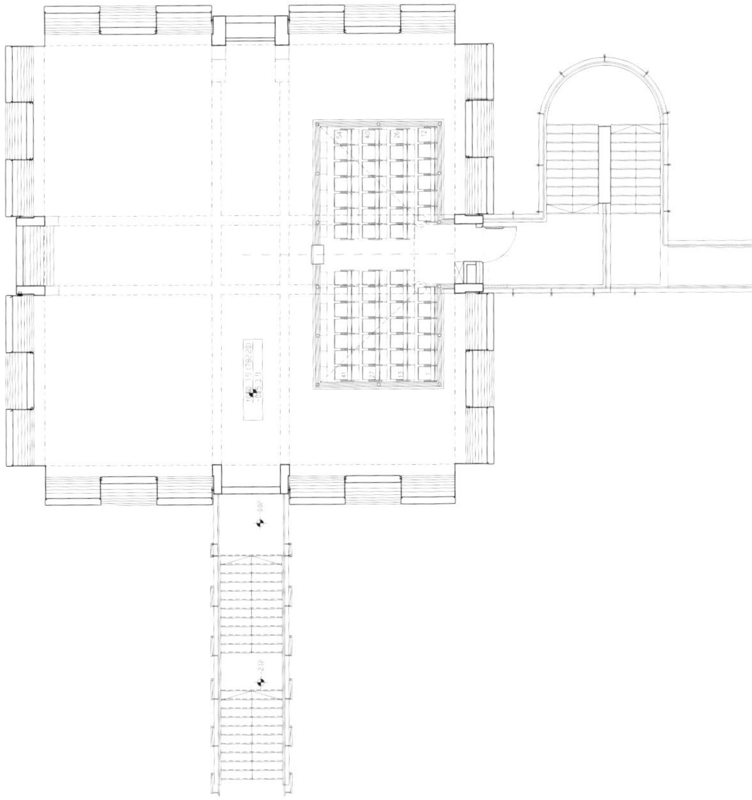

Mezzanine Floor

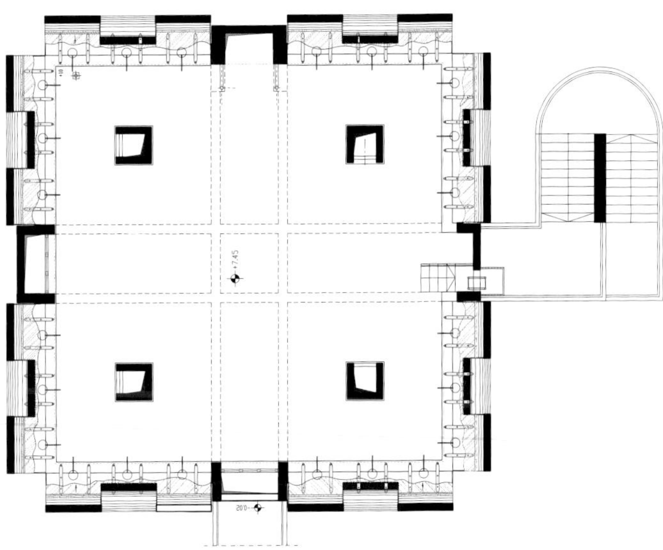

Roof Floor

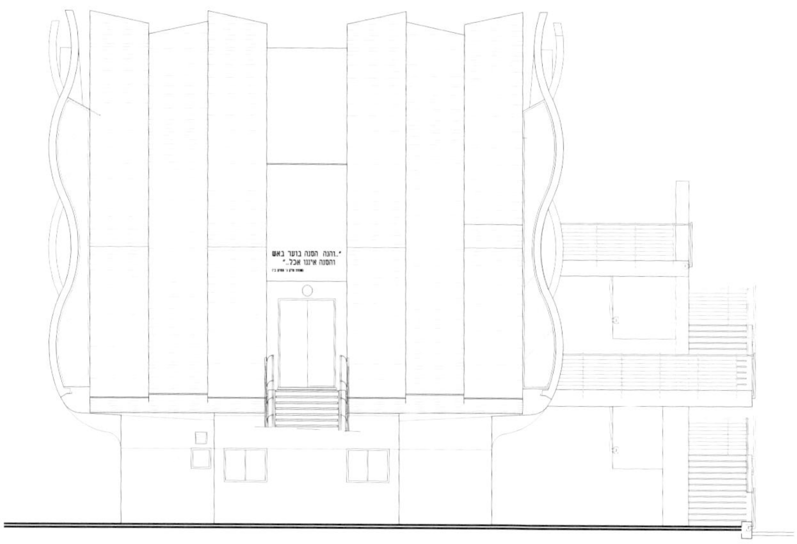

South Façade

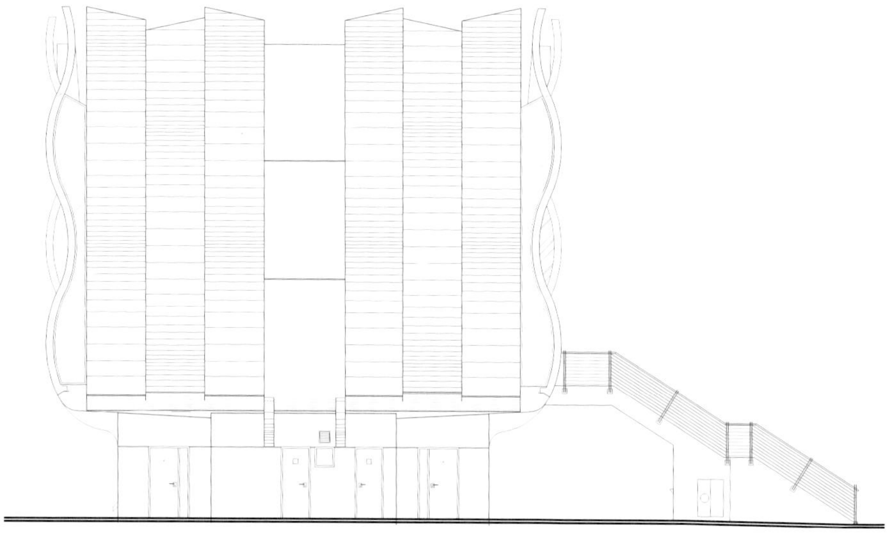

West Façade

North Façade

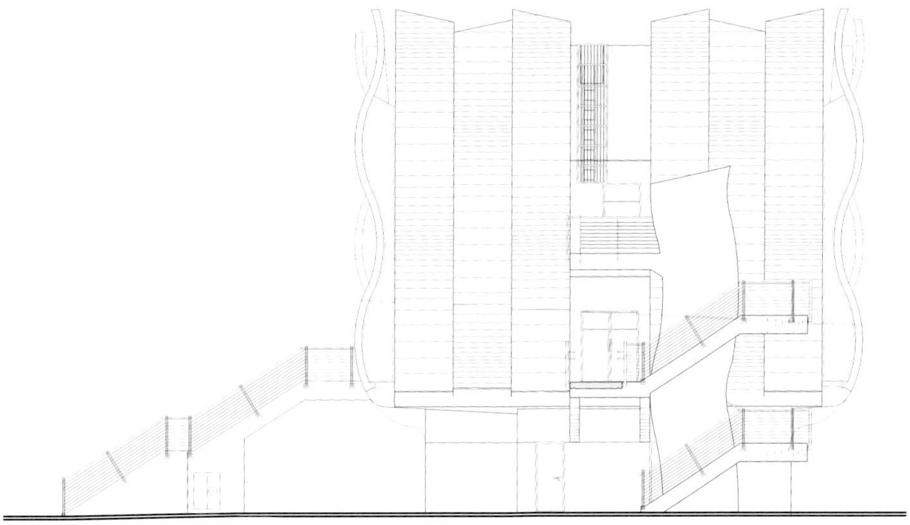

East Façade

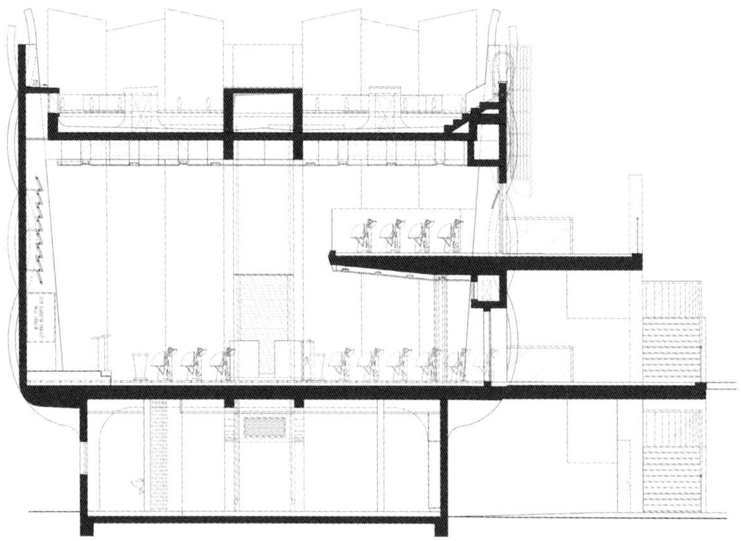

Section Looking South

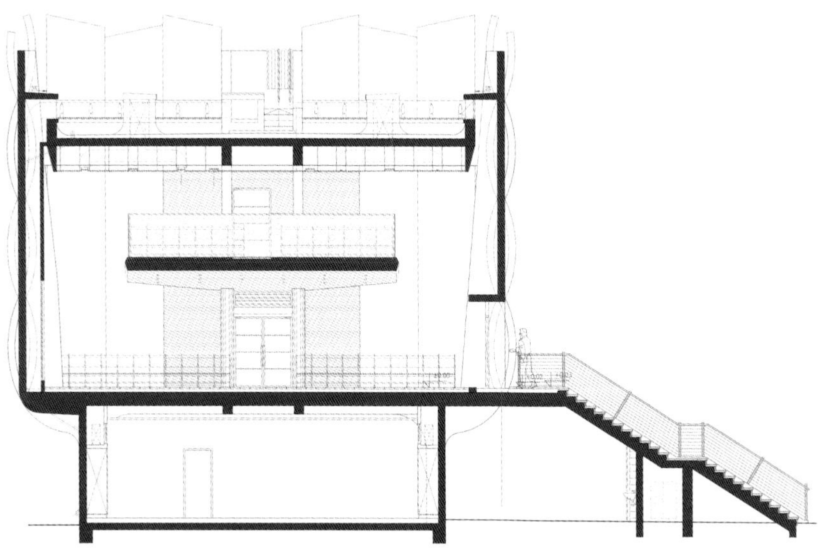

Section Looking West

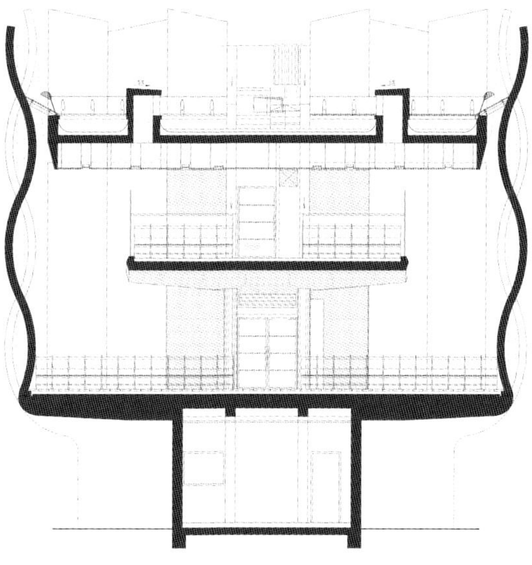

Section Looking East

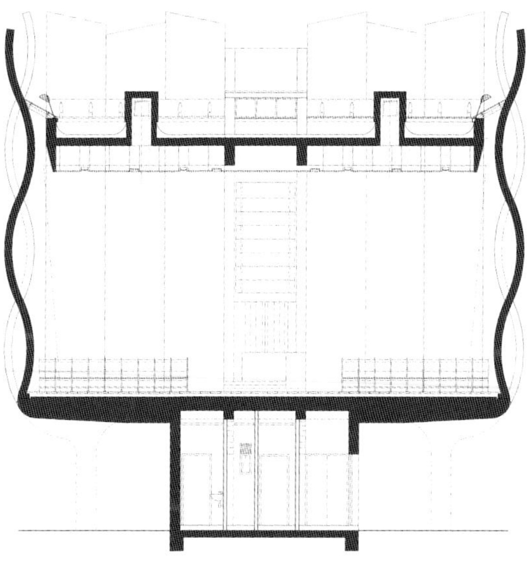

Section Looking North

CONSTRUCTION

WORKING DRAWINGS

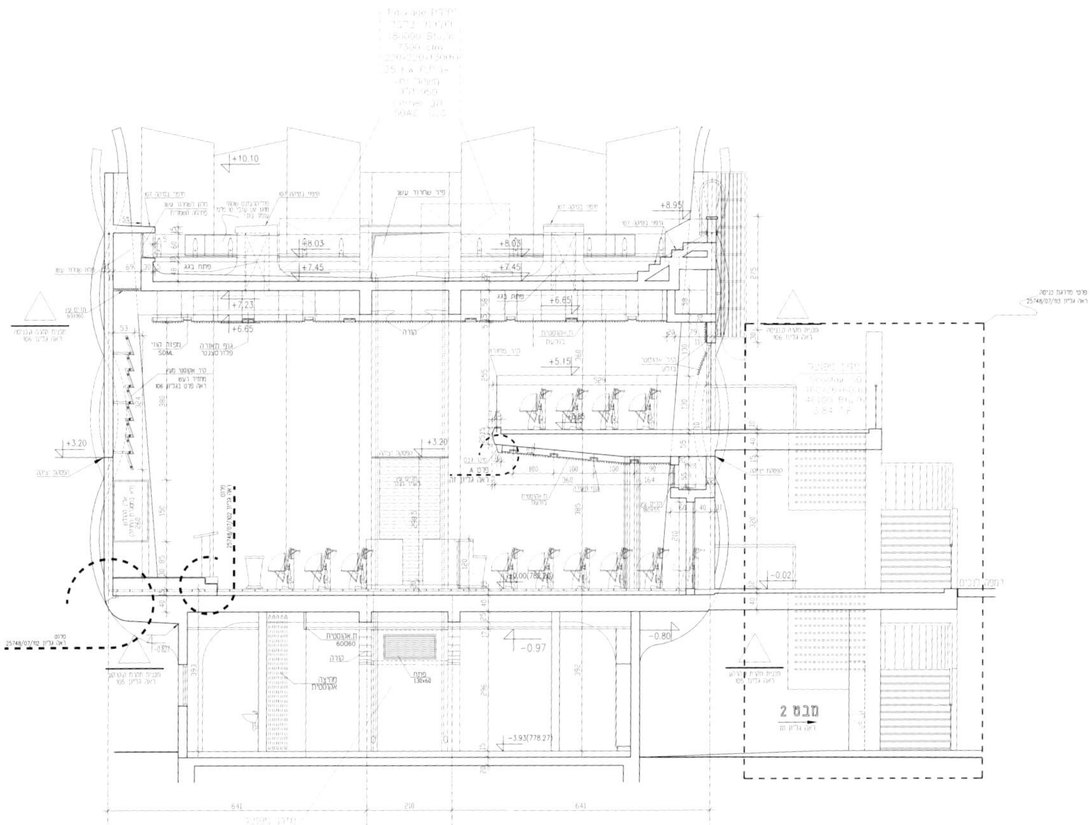
+10.10
+8.95
+8.03
+7.45
+7.23
+6.85
+6.65
+5.15
+3.20
-0.02
-0.80
-0.97
-3.93(778.27)
מבט 2
641
210
641
D
C
B
A
חתך 1-1

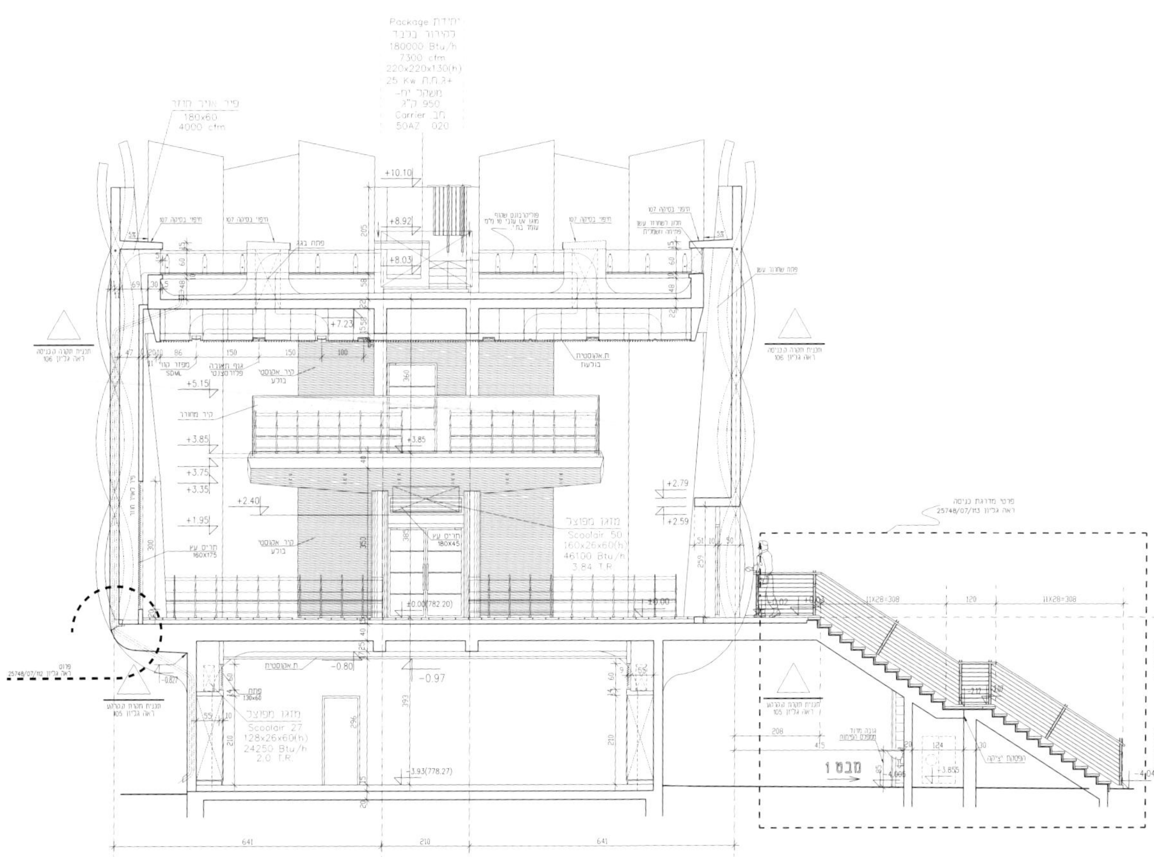
Package יחידת
180000 Btu/h
7300 cfm
220x220x130(h)
Carrier
50AZ 020
+10.10
+8.92
+8.03
+7.23
+5.15
+3.85
+3.75
+3.35
+2.79
+2.59
+2.40
+1.95
±0.00(782.20)
-0.80
-0.97
-3.93(778.27)
Scoolair 50
160x26x60(h)
46100 Btu/h
3.84 T.R.
Scoolair 27
128x26x60(h)
24250 Btu/h
2.0 T.R.
מבט 1
641
210
641
4
3
2
1
חתך 2-2

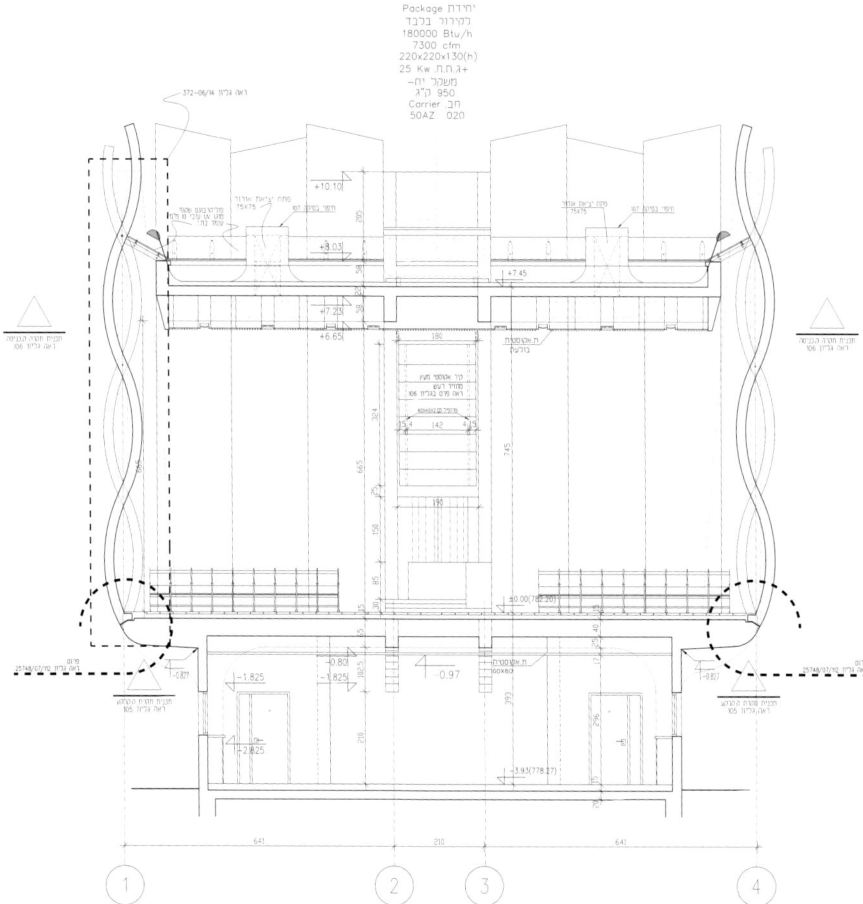
Package
180000 Btu/h
7300 cfm
220x220x130(h)
950
Carrier
50AZ 020
+10.10
+8.03
+7.45
+7.23
+6.65
±0.00(782.20)
-3.93(778.27)
641
210
641
1
2
3
4

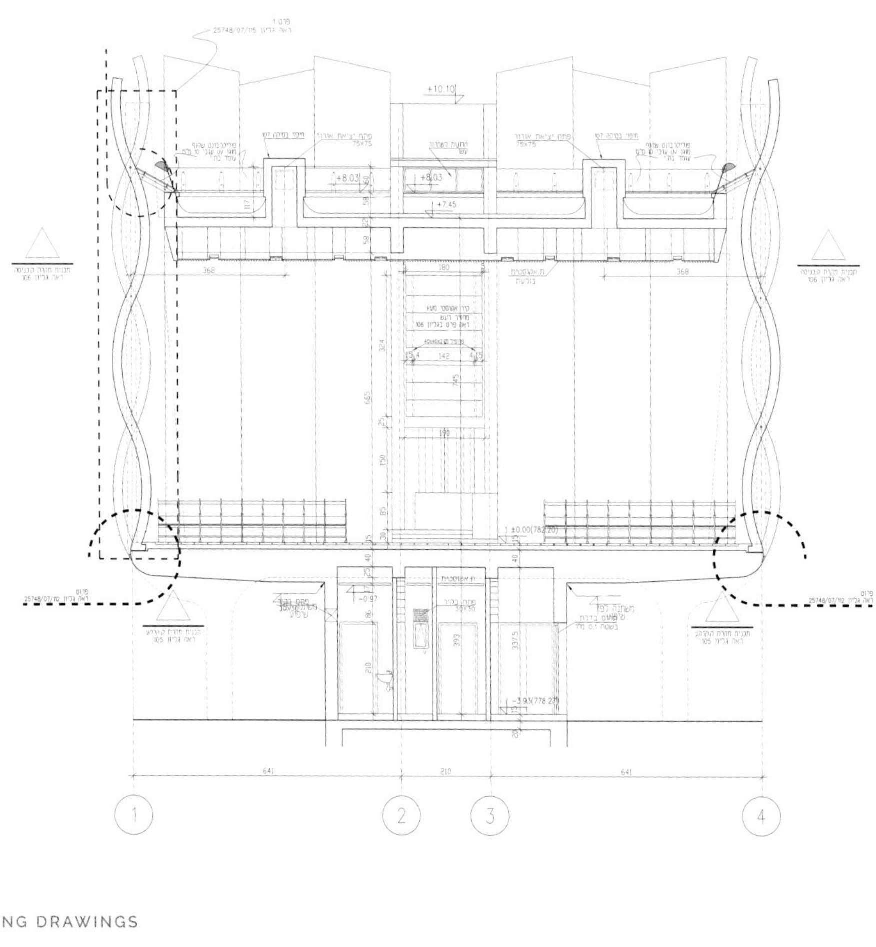
+10.10
+8.03
+7.45
368
368
±0.00(782.20)
-3.93(778.27)
641
210
641
1
2
3
4

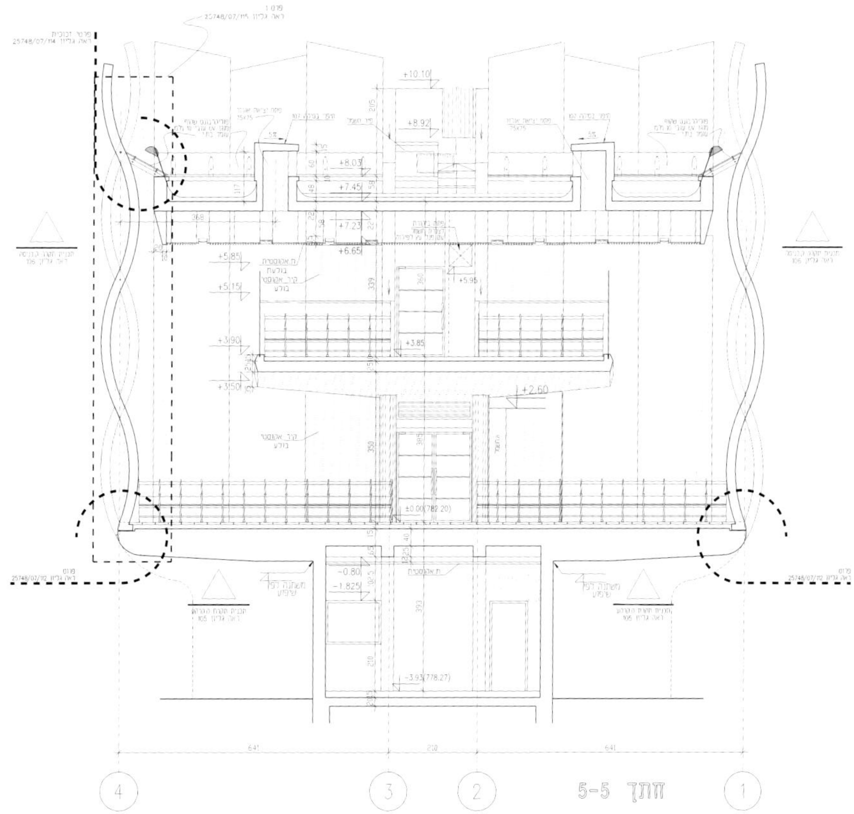
4
3
2
חתך 5-5
1

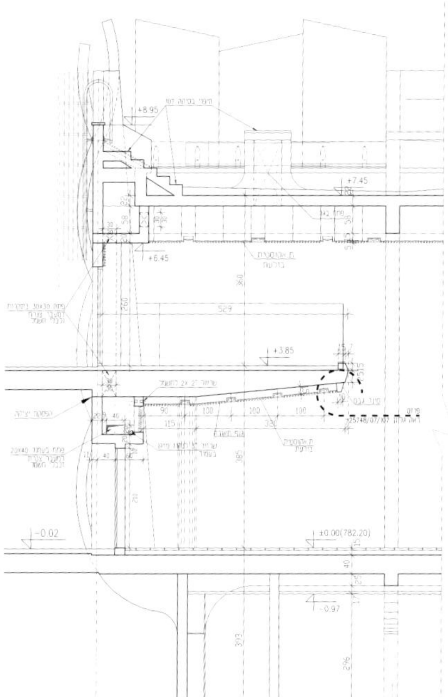
A
חתך 6-6
B

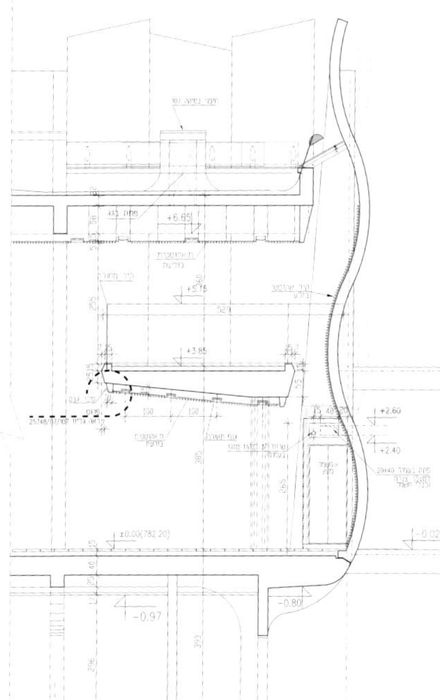
B
חתך 7-7
A

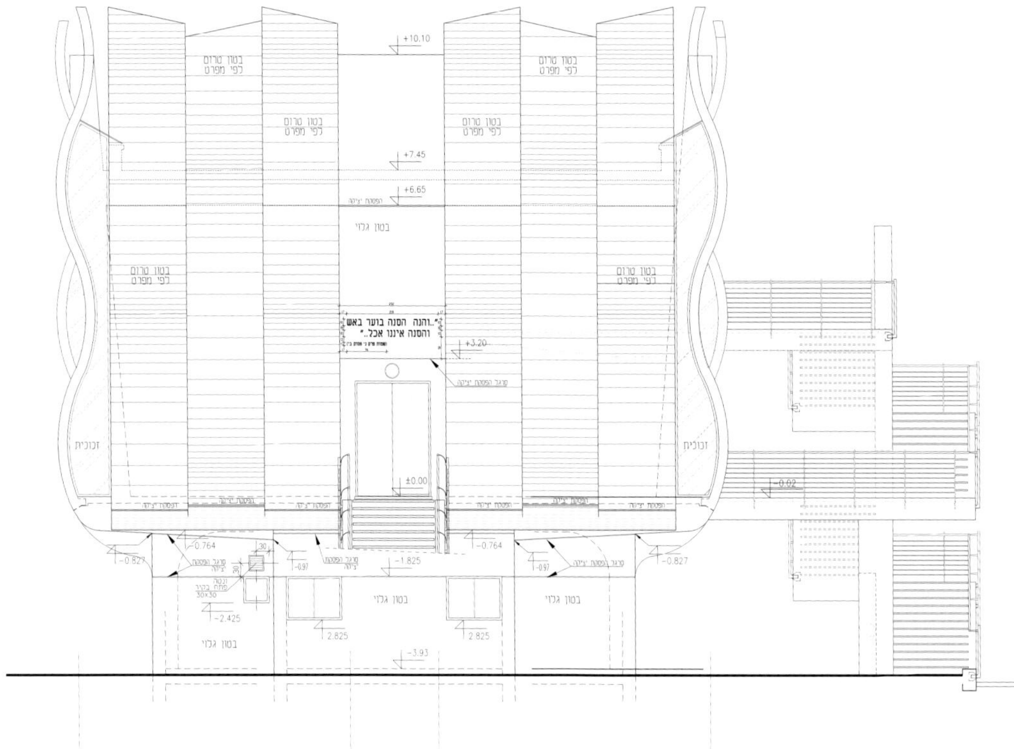

חזית D - A

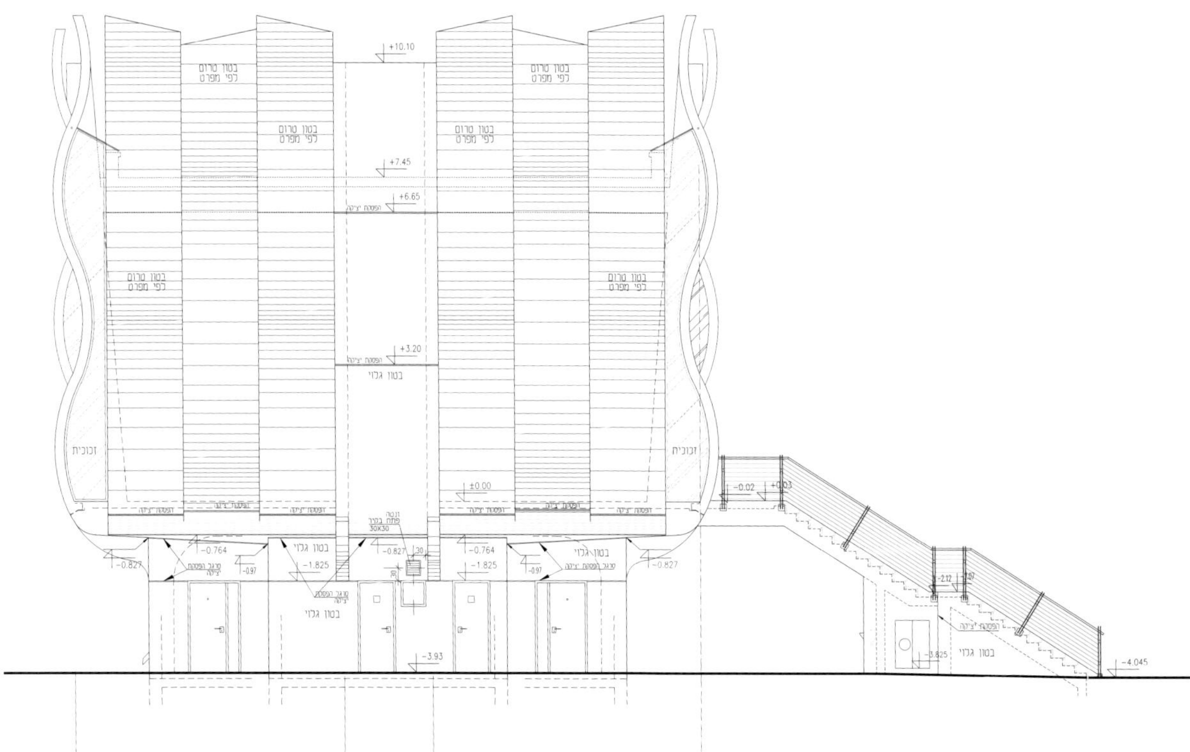

חזית 4-1

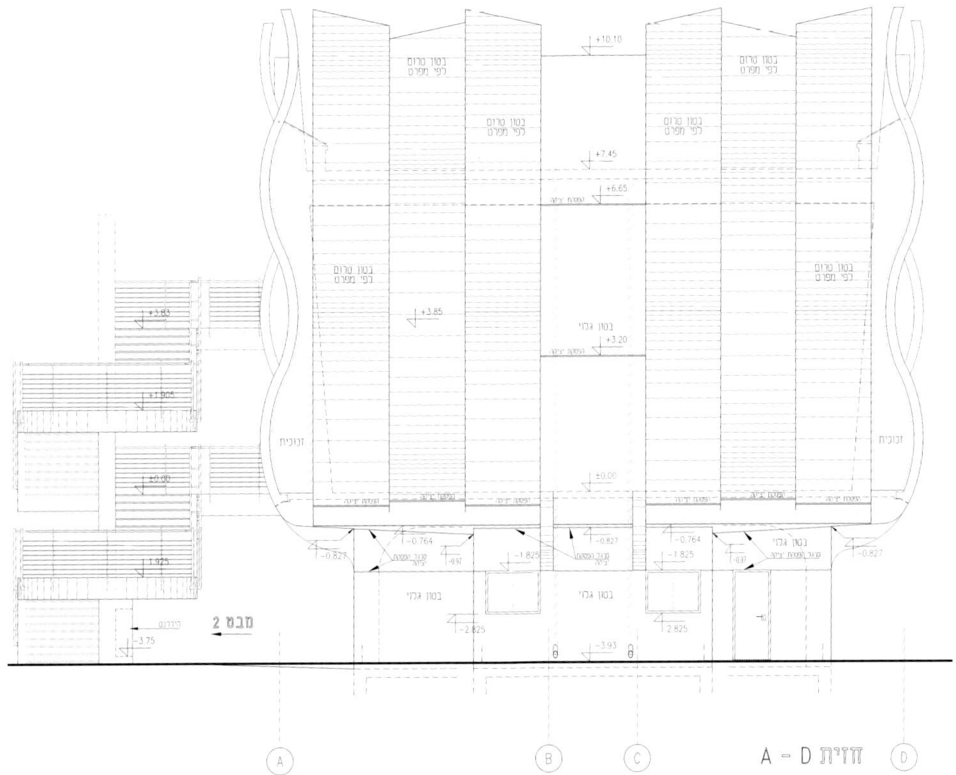

חזית A - D

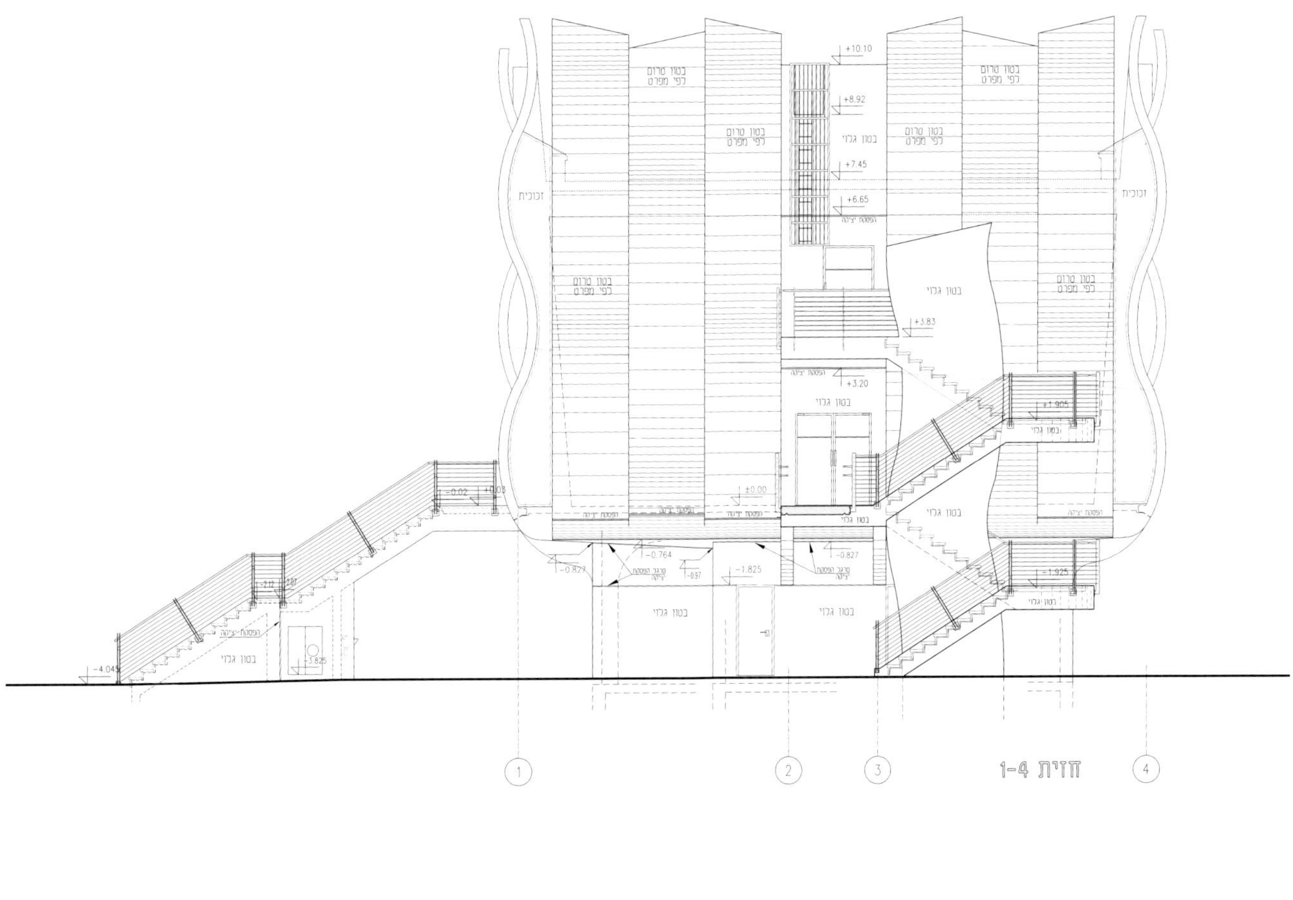

חזית 1-4

יש להוסיף רשימת ריכוז של כלל התוכניות בהגשה (נספח א׳)

עדכונים ושינויים (מהדורות)

שינוי	תאריך	מהות העדכון/השינוי
2	28.07.2008	תקון הדרנטים וכיורי נטילת ידים מתחת למדרגות
4	17.12.2008	פרוט שרותים

רשימת תפוצה

מקבל / תאריך	מנהל הפרויקט	מתאם	קבלן	לקוח	אדריכלות	קונסטרוקציה	חשמל	מכונות	אינסטלציה	פיתוח ונ״ע	תנועה	מיזוג אוויר	בטיחות	נוף	תקשורת	כמא״י	אקוסטיקה	מפקוח משה״בט
25.2.2008						1												
04.12.2008									1									
28.07.2008	1					1												1
11.08.2008																		4
08.12.2008							1					1						
17.12.2008	1																	5
12.02.02009																		3
17.02.02009						1												
21.09.2009																		1

אישור תכנון (יש למלא בכתב יד\חותמת)

מס״ד	שם	תפקיד	תאריך	חתימה
1	ויקי ליכשטיין	מנהל הפרויקט		
2	דניאל רוד	רע״ן		
3	מז״י ענף תשתיות ובינוי	לקוח		
4				

מרכז הבינוי / ענף הדרום

ביקורת קבלה - מסמכי תכנון

מאושר ע״י: ____________ חתימה: ____________ תאריך: ________

המבצע אחראי לבדיקת המידות ולהתאמתן במקום. על המבצע לבקר את כל המידות ולהודיע למשרד המתכנן על כל טעות או אי - התאמה.

לעיון ○ לאישור ○ למכרז ○ לביצוע ●

מסי גיליון: 101 **מהדורה:** 3

קנ״מ: 1:50 **תאריך:** 17.12.2008

מס׳ התכנית

מס׳ שוטף		סוג	שנה		מס׳ הפרויקט					
1	0	1	7	0	8	4	7	5	2	P

שם התוכנית

תכנית קומת קרקע

שם הפרויקט

בית כנסת בהייד 1

שם המשימה

בית כנסת בהייד 1 ליביי

שם היחידה

בית כנסת בהייד 1 ליביי

שם המחנה או המ״ק (חל איסור לרשום את שניהם יחד)

1000771

המתכנן:

ארמון
אדריכלים ומתכנני ערים בע״מ
ARMON ARCHITECTS & TOWN PLANNERS
רח׳ יהודה הנחתום 4 באר שבע ת.ד.1520
ט״ל: 08-6287668/9 פקס: 08-6287667

מכון התקנים הישראלי
מכון התקנים הישראלי

ערך: אלי ארמון **בקר:** בני סבדוש

שרטט: טניה / עדית **אשר:** אלי ארמון

סווג בטחוני: ב ל מ ׳ ׳ ס

מערך הבינוי בונה היום את צה״ל של המחר

כל המוסר תוכן מסמך זה , כולו או קצתו לידיעת אנשים שאינם מוסמכים לכך עובר על חוקי ביטחון המדינה. כל המוצא מסמך זה נדרש למוסרו לתחנה הקרובה ביותר של משטרת ישראל או המשטרה הצבאית

מרכז הבינוי 5600
ענף הדרום

טבלת ציפויים וחומרי גמר

קבוצת גמר	הערות :	ריצוף מיקום	ריצוף כללי	ריצוף הדגשה	קירות גבה	קירות כללי	קירות הדגשה	תקרה	דלתות כנף כללי	דלתות כנף הדגשה	דלתות משקוף
1	כיתת לימוד		טרצו CER-1		לכל הגובה	סופרקריל 2000 PNT-1		מינרלית 60X60	פלדה PNT-3		מתכת PNT-2
2	משרד		טרצו CER-1		לכל הגובה	סופרקריל 2000 PNT-2		מינרלית 60X60	פלדה PNT-3		מתכת PNT-2
3	שרותי גברים		קרמיקה CER-2		H=1.10	חרסינה / לבן	H=1.10	מגשי פח לאמחורר	דלת כניסה: מתכת / דלת חדר השרותים: עץ		דלת כניסה: מתכת / דלת חדר השרותים: מתכת
3	שרותי נשים		קרמיקה CER-2		H=1.10	חרסינה / לבן	H=1.10	מגשי פח לאמחורר	דלת כניסה: מתכת / דלת חדר השרותים: עץ		דלת כניסה: מתכת / דלת חדר השרותים: מתכת
4	מחסן		טרצו CER-3		לכל הגובה	סופרקריל 2000 PNT-2			פלדה PNT-3		מתכת PNT-2

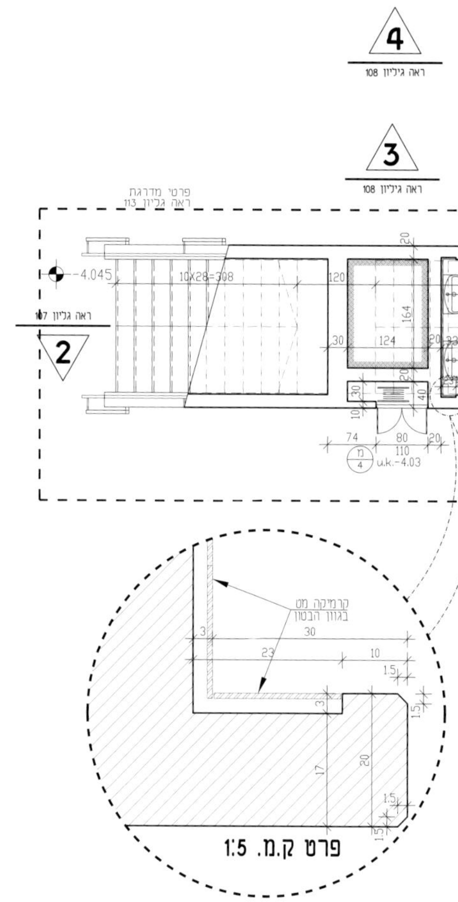

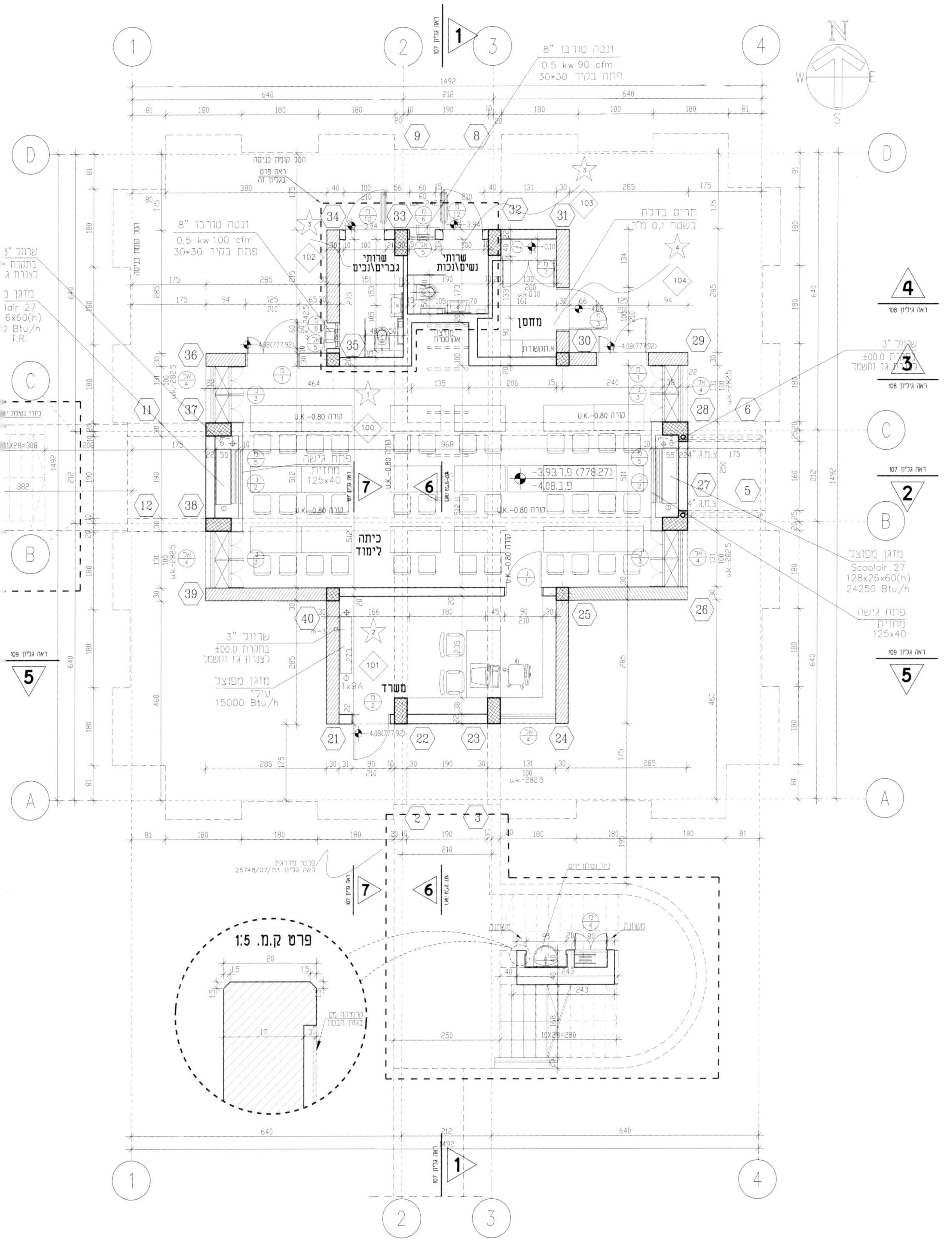
כיתה לימוד
משרד
מחסן
שרותי גברים\נכים
שרותי נשים\נכות
פרט ק.מ. 1:5
מזגן מפוצל
Scoolair 27
128x26x60(h)
24250 Btu/h
פתח גישה מחזית 125x40
ונטה טורבו "8
0.5 kw 90 cfm
פתח בקיר 30*30
ונטה טורבו "8
0.5 kw 100 cfm
פתח בקיר 30*30
תריס בדלת בשטח 0.1 מ"ר
מזגן מפוצל
15000 Btu/h

יש להוסיף רשימת ריכוז של כלל התוכניות בהגשה (נספח א׳)

עדכונים ושינויים (מהדורות)

שינוי	תאריך	מהות העדכון/השינוי
2	12.05.2008	שינוי ריהוט באולם תפילת הגברים
3	22.07.2008	תיקוני ריהוט באולם תפילת הגברים
4	11.08.2008	תוספת פרטי משקופים
5	07.09.2008	שינוי דלתות א.הקודש ותוספת כסאות
6	15.09.2008	תקון דלת יציאה צדדית תוספת סימוני "נ"ים" לרשימת נגרות
7	28.10.2008	העתקת א.חשמל לצדן השני של עמוד מס׳ 2 תוספת חתכים 6-6, 7-7
8	16.11.2008	שינוי מידות א.חשמל נ-7
9	14.12.2008	פירוט במת ארון הקודש

רשימת תפוצה

מקבל / תאריך	מנהל הפרויקט	מתאם	קבלן	לקוח	אדריכלות	קונסטרוקציה	חשמל	מכונות	אינסטלציה	פיתוח ונו"ף	תנועה	מיזוג אויר	בטיחות	נו"ף	תקשורת	כמאי	אקוסטיקה	מפקוח משהב"ט
25.2.2008						1												
04.12.2008									1									
04.11.2008	1					1												5
08.12.2008							1					1						
17.12.2008	1																	5
12.02.02009																		3
17.02.02009						1												
21.09.2009																		1

אישור תכנון (יש למלא בכתב יד\חותמת)

מס״ד	שם	תפקיד	תאריך	חתימה
1	ויקי ליכשטיין	מנהל הפרויקט		
2	דניאל רוד	רע״ן		
3	מז״י ענף תשתיות ובינוי	לקוח		
4				

מרכז הבינוי / ענף הדרום

ביקורת קבלה - מסמכי תכנון

מאושר ע״י: ____________

חתימה: ____________ תאריך: ________

המבצע אחראי לבדיקת המידות ולהתאמתן במקום. על המבצע לבקר את כל המידות ולהודיע למשרד המתכנן על כל טעות או אי - התאמה.

לעיון ○ לאישור ○ למכרז ○ לביצוע ●

מסי גיליון: 102 **מהדורה:** 3

קנ״מ: 1:50 **תאריך:** 17.12.2008

מס׳ התכנית

מס׳ שוטף	סוג	שנה	מס׳ הפרויקט	
0 2	1	0 7	2 5 7 4 8	P

שם התוכנית

תכנית קומת כניסה ביכניים

שם הפרויקט

בית כנסת בהייד 1

שם המשימה

בית כנסת בהייד 1 ליביי

שם היחידה

בית כנסת בהייד 1 ליביי

שם המחנה או המי״ק (חל איסור לרשום את שניהם יחד)

1000771

המתכנן:

מכון התקנים הישראלי

ארמון

אדריכלים ומתכנני ערים בע״מ

ARMON ARCHITECTS & TOWN PLANNERS

רח׳ יהודה הנחתום 4 באר שבע ת.ד.1520

ט״ל: 08-6287668/9 פקס: 08-6287667

ערך: אלי ארמון **בקר:** בני סבדוש

שרטט: טניה / עדית **אשר:** אלי ארמון

סווג בטחוני: ב ל מ ׳ ׳ ס

כל המוסר תוכן מסמך זה, כולו או קצתו לידיעת אנשים שאינם מוסמכים לכך עובר על חוקי ביטחון המדינה. כל המוצא מסמך זה נדרש למוסרו לתחנה הקרובה ביותר של משטרת ישראל או המשטרה הצבאית

מערך הבינוי בונה היום

את צה״ל של המחר

מרכז הבינוי 5600

ענף הדרום

קבוצת גמר	הערות:	ריצוף כללי	גבה	קירות כללי	תקרה	דלתות כנף כללי	דלתות כנף הדגשה	דלתות משקוף
5	אולם תפילה לגברים	גרניט פורצלן אנטי סליפ דרגה 10 או אופציה: אבן מצפה גון צהוב דרגה 3 מלוטש מבריק	לכל הגובה	בטון חשוף	אקוסטית למלות פח	אלומיניום PNT-4	אלומיניום PNT-4	
6	מדרגות	גרניט פורצלן אנטי סליפ דרגה 10 או אופציה: אבן מצפה גון צהוב בעבוד טלטיש עדין	לכל הגובה	בטון חשוף	מעקה: מתכת משולב בנירוסטה			

טבלת ציפויים וחומרי גמר

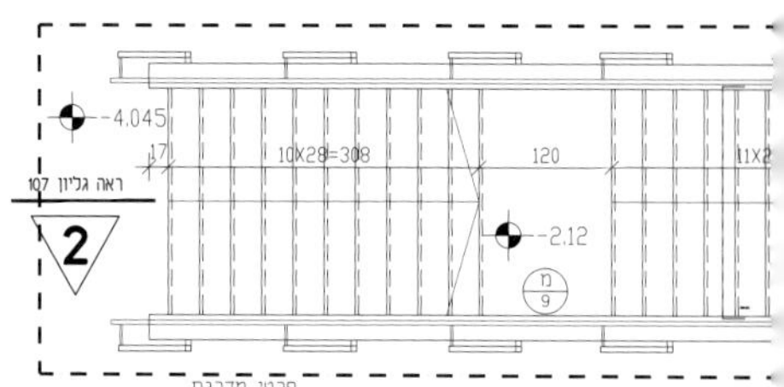

פרטי מדרגת
ראה גליון 113

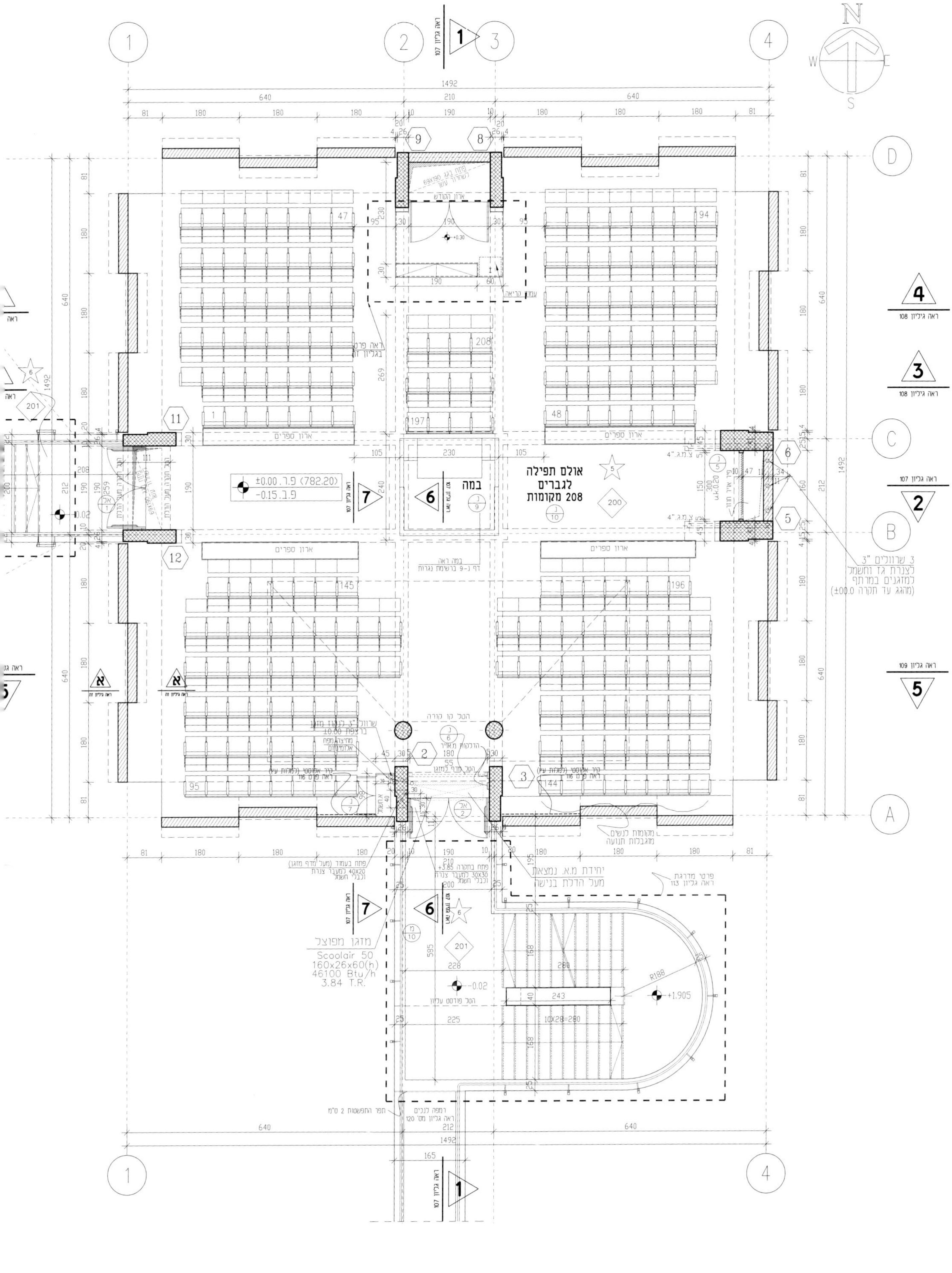
אולם תפילה
לגברים
208 מקומות
במה
ארון ספרים
מזגן מפוצל
Scoolair 50
160x26x60(h)
46100 Btu/h
3.84 T.R.

טבלת ציפויים וחומרי גמר

קבוצת גמר	הערות :	ריצוף		קירות		תקרה	דלתות		
		כללי		גבה	כללי		כנף כללי	כנף הדגשה	משקוף
5	עזרת נשים	גרניט פורצלן אנטי סליפ דרגה 10 או אופציה: אבן מצפה גון צהוב בעבוד טלטיש עדין		כבר הגובה	בטון חשוף	אקוסטית עץ / מעקה במתחת	אלומניום		אלומניום
							PNT-4		PNT-4

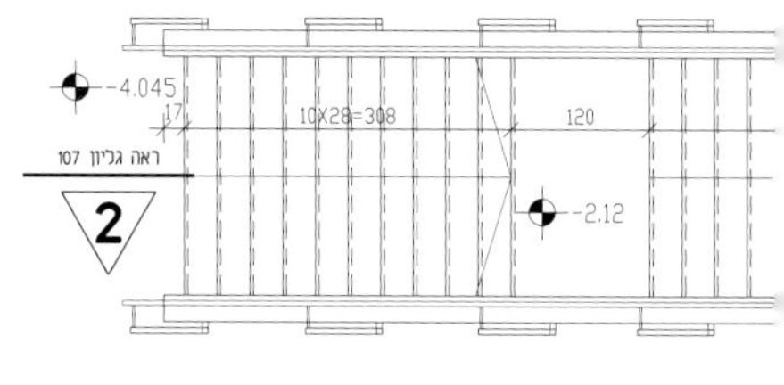

יש להוסיף רשימת ריכוז של כלל התוכניות בהגשה (נספח א׳)

עדכונים ושינויים (מהדורות)

שינוי	תאריך	מהות העדכון/השינוי
2	11.08.2008	תוספת פרט משקוף
3	28.10.2008	עדכון פיר חשמל תוספת חתכים 6-6, 7-7
4	29.10.2008	תוספת פרט A (פרט חיבור זכוכית לאלמנט טרומי)
5	30.10.2008	הגדלת כמות הכסאות בע.נשים ל-54
6	10.11.2008	סימון קירות פיר חשמל לבטון
7	16.11.2008	תיקון פרט A
8	26.11.2008	תוספת פרט B

רשימת תפוצה

מקבל / תאריך	מנהל הפרויקט	מתאם	קבלן	לקוח	אדריכלות	קונסטרוקציה	חשמל	מכונות	אינסטלציה	פיתוח ונו״ע	תנועה	מיזוג אוויר	בטיחות	נוף	תקשורת	כמאי	אקוסטיקה	תפקוד משהב״ם
25.2.2008						1												
04.12.2008									1									
04.11.2008	1					1												5
08.12.2008							1					1						
17.12.2008	1																	5
12.02.02009																		3
17.02.02009						1												
21.09.2009																		1

אישור תכנון (יש למלא בכתב יד\חותמת)

מס״ד	שם	תפקיד	תאריך	חתימה
1	ויקי ליכשטיין	מנהל הפרויקט		
2	דניאל רוד	רע״ן		
3	מז״י ענף תשתיות ובינוי	לקוח		
4				

מרכז הבינוי / ענף הדרום

ביקורת קבלה - מסמכי תכנון

מאושר ע״י: ____________

חתימה: ____________ תאריך: ________

המבצע אחראי לבדיקת המידות ולהתאמתן במקום. על המבצע לבקר את כל המידות ולהודיע למשרד המתכנן על כל טעות או אי - התאמה.

לעיון ○ לאישור ○ למכרז ○ לביצוע ●

מסי גיליון: 103 **מהדורה:** 3

קנ״מ: 1:50 **תאריך:** 17.12.2008

מס׳ התכנית

מס׳ שוטף		סוג	שנה		מס׳ הפרויקט					
3	0	1	7	0	8	4	7	5	2	P

שם התוכנית

תכנית קומת עזרת נשים

שם הפרויקט

בית כנסת בהייד 1

שם המשימה

בית כנסת בהייד 1 ליביי

שם היחידה

בית כנסת בהייד 1 ליביי

שם המחנה או המ״ק (חל איסור לרשום את שניהם יחד)

1000771

המתכנן:

ארמון

אדריכלים ומתכנני ערים בע״מ

ARMON ARCHITECTS & TOWN PLANNERS

רח׳ יהודה הנחתום 4 באר שבע ת.ד.1520

ט״ל: 08-6287668/9 פקס: 08-6287667

מכון התקנים הישראלי

מכון התקנים הישראלי ISO 9001 2000

ערך: אלי ארמון **בקר:** בני סבדוש

שרטט: טניה / עדית **אשר:** אלי ארמון

סווג בטחוני: ב ל מ ׳ ׳ ס

כל המוסר תוכן מסמך זה , כולו או קצתו לידיעת אנשים שאינם מוסמכים לכך עובר על חוקי ביטחון המדינה. כל המוצא מסמך זה נדרש למוסרו לתחנה הקרובה ביותר של משטרת ישראל או המשטרה הצבאית

מערך הבינוי בונה היום את צה״ל של המחר

מרכז הבינוי 5600

ענף הדרום

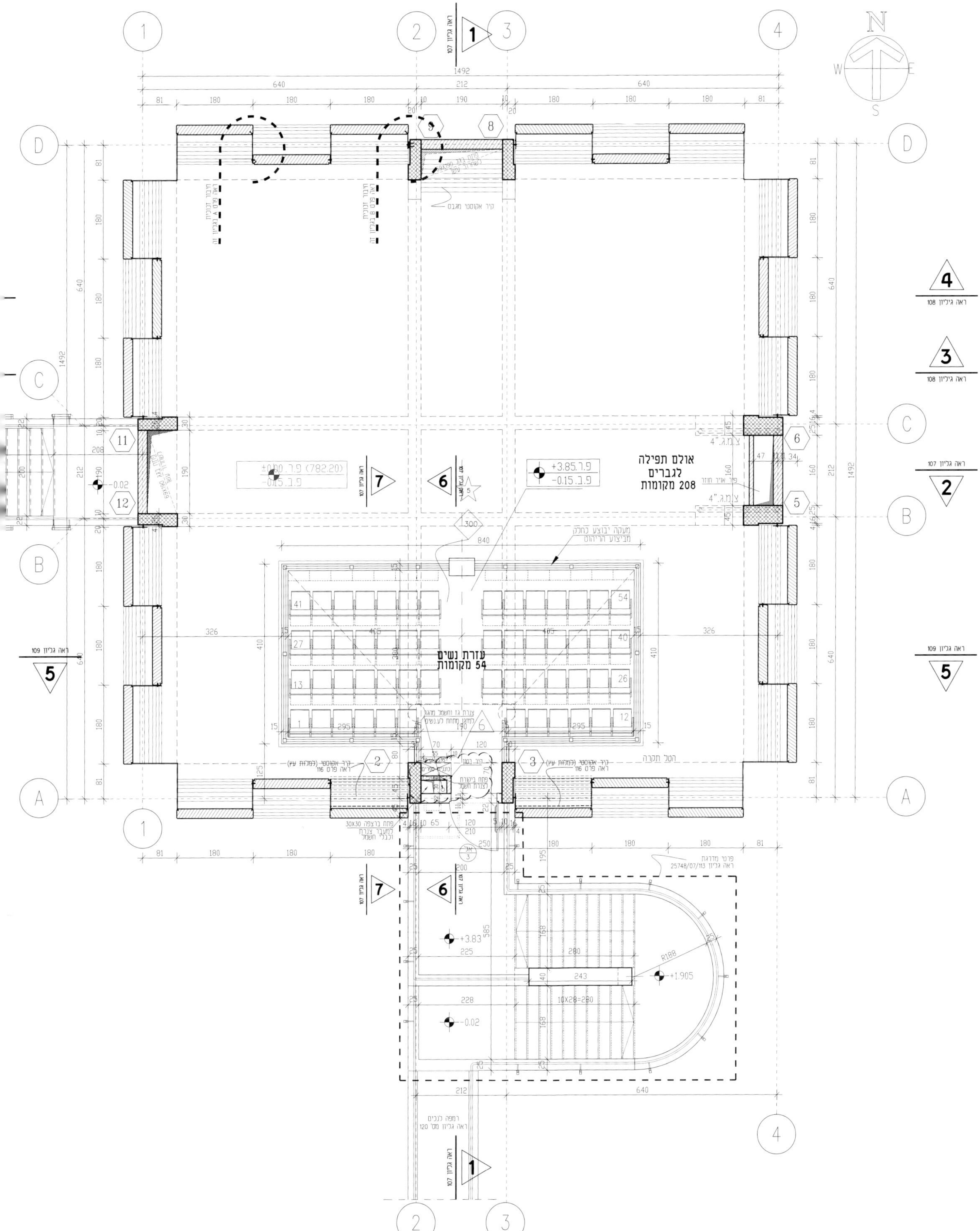
אולם תפילה
לגברים
208 מקומות
עזרת נשים
54 מקומות
ראה גליון 107
ראה גליון 108
ראה גליון 109
N
W
E
S
1492
640
212
640

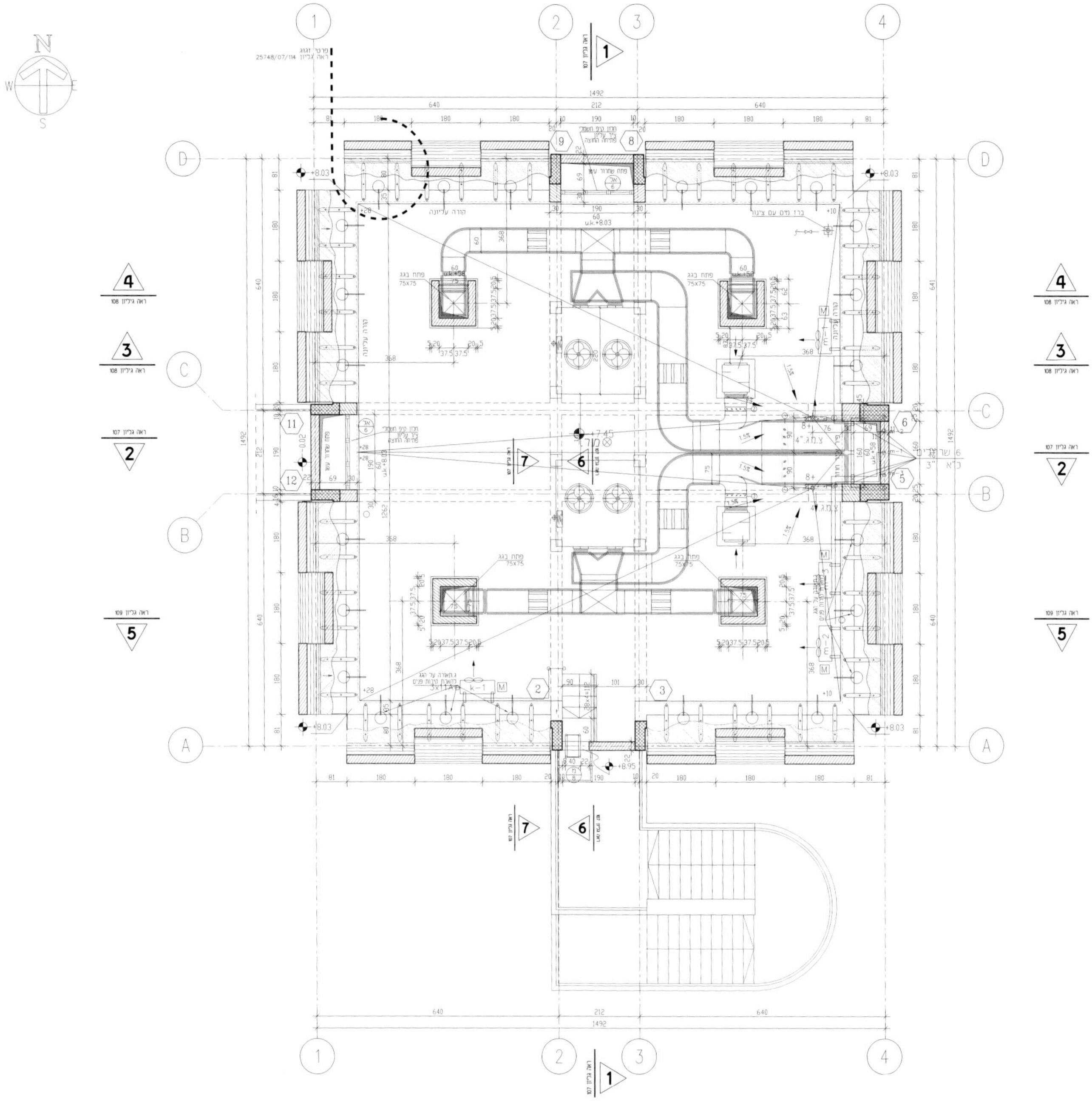

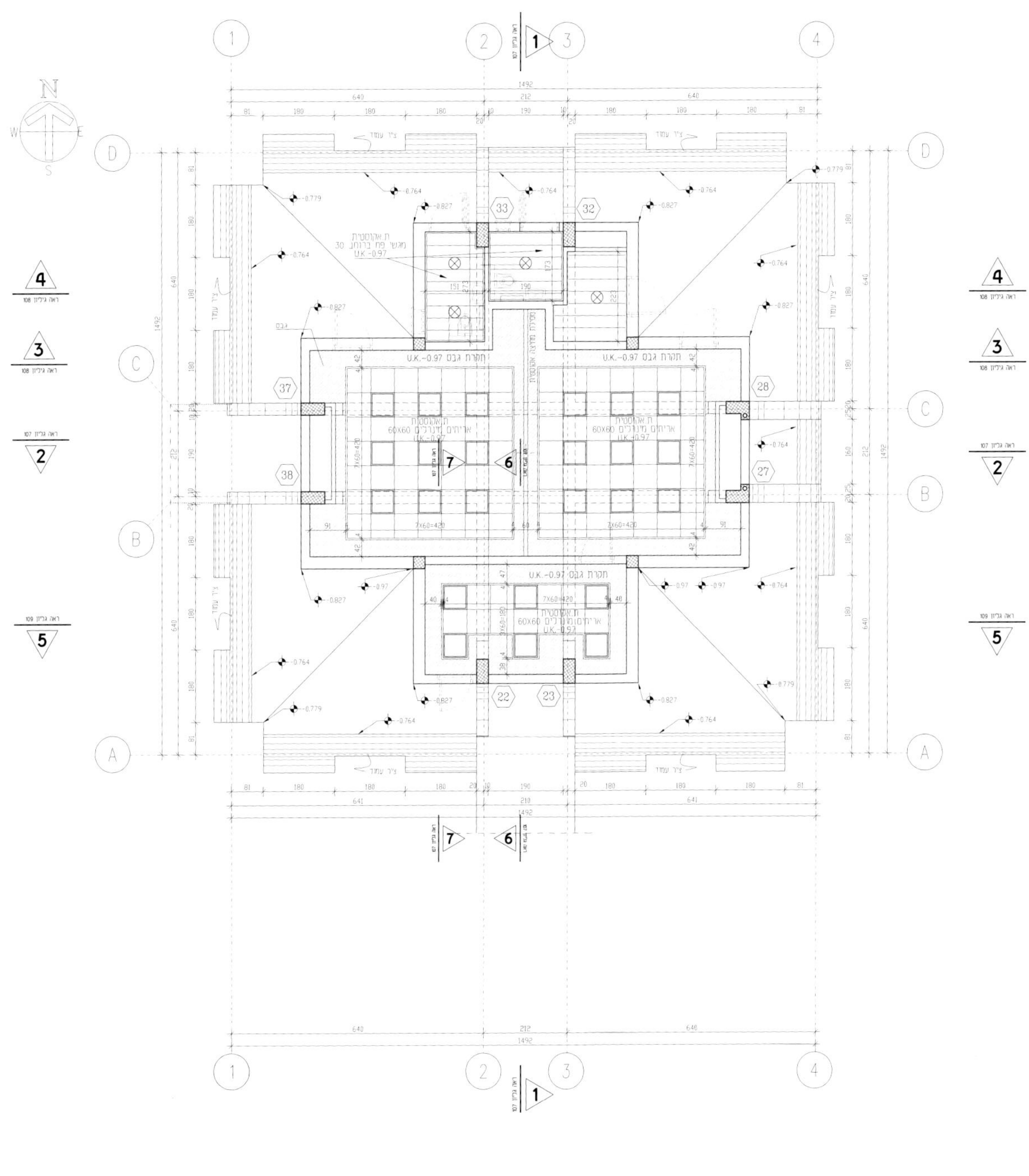

עדכונים ושינויים (מהדורות)

שינוי	תאריך	מהות העדכון/השינוי
1	24.03.2009	שינוי פרט קיר אקוסטי
2	05.05.2009	שינוי סידור הלמלות בתקרת אולם התפילה

רשימת תפוצה

מקבל / תאריך	מנהל הפרויקט	מתאם	קבלן	לקוח	אדריכלות	קונסטרוקציה	חשמל	מכונות	אינסטלציה	פיתוח וגינון	תנועה	מיזוג אויר	בטיחות	נוף	תקשורת	כמאי	אקוסטיקה	מפקחת משהב"ט
25.2.2008						1												
04.12.2008									1									
08.12.2008							1					1						
17.12.2008	1																	5
[illegible]																		[illegible]
[illegible]			2			1												
05.05.2009							1											
10.05.2009	1											1						5
21.09.2009																		1

אישור תכנון (יש למלא בכתב יד\חותמת)

מס"ד	שם	תפקיד	תאריך	חתימה
1	ויקי ליכשטיין	מנהל הפרויקט		
2	דניאל רוד	רע"ן		
3	מז"י ענף תשתיות ובינוי	לקוח		
4				

מרכז הבינוי / ענף הדרום

ביקורת קבלה - מסמכי תכנון

מאושר ע"י: ________

חתימה: ________ תאריך: ________

המבצע אחראי לבדיקת המידות ולהתאמתן במקום. על המבצע לבקר את כל המידות ולהודיע למשרד המתכנן על כל טעות או אי - התאמה.

לעיון ○ לאישור ○ למכרז ○ לביצוע ●

מסי גיליון: 106 **מהדורה:** 3

קנ"מ: 1:50 **תאריך:** 17.12.2008

מס' התכנית

מס' שוטף	סוג	שנה	מס' הפרויקט	
6 0	1	7 0	8 4 7 5 2	P

שם התוכנית

תכנית תקרות ק.כניסה ועזרת נשים
חפוי קירות בעץ אקוסטי

שם הפרויקט

בית כנסת בהייד 1

שם המשימה

בית כנסת בהייד 1 ליביי

שם היחידה

בית כנסת בהייד 1 ליביי

שם המחנה או המ"ק (חל איסור לרשום את שניהם יחד)

1000771

המתכנן:

ארמון
אדריכלים ומתכנני ערים בע"מ
ARMON ARCHITECTS & TOWN PLANNERS
רח' יהודה הנחתום 4 באר שבע ת.ד.1520
ט"ל: 08-6287668/9 פקס: 08-6287667

מכון התקנים הישראלי

ערך: אלי ארמון **בקר:** בני סבדוש

שרטט: טניה / עדית **אשר:** אלי ארמון

סווג בטחוני: ב ל מ ' ' ס

כל המוסר תוכן מסמך זה, כולו או קצתו לידיעת אנשים שאינם מוסמכים לכך עובר על חוקי ביטחון המדינה. כל המוצא מסמך זה נדרש למוסרו לתחנה הקרובה ביותר של משטרת ישראל או המשטרה הצבאית

מערך הבינוי בונה היום את צה"ל של המחר

מרכז הבינוי 5600
ענף הדרום

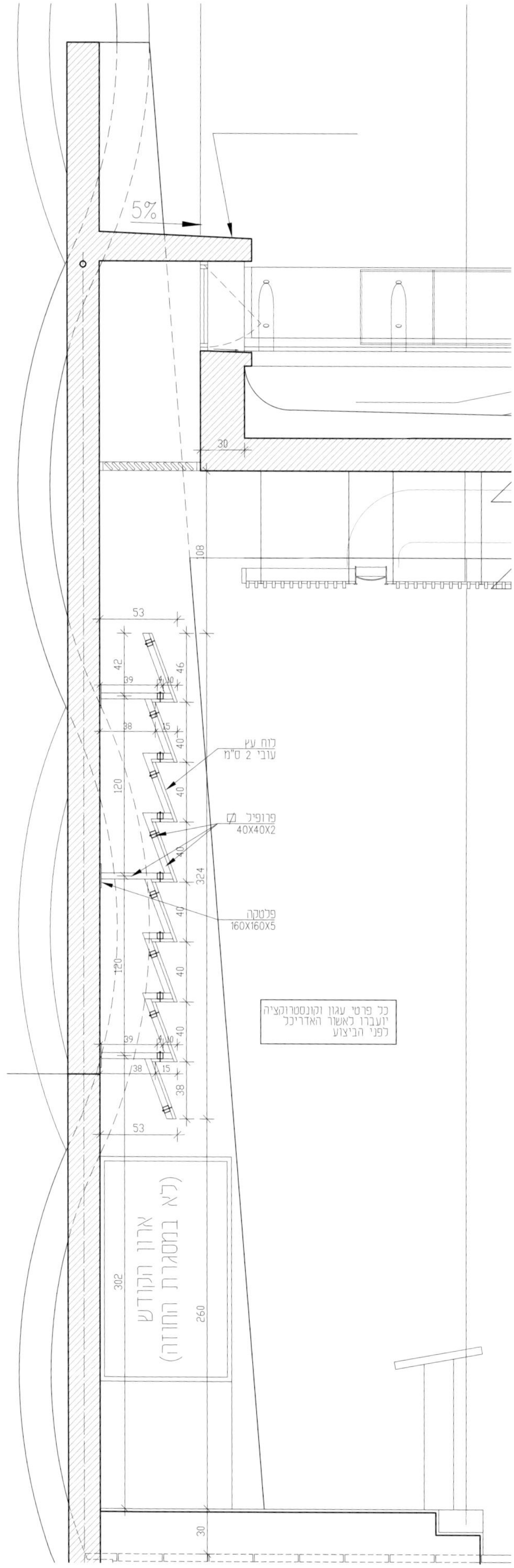

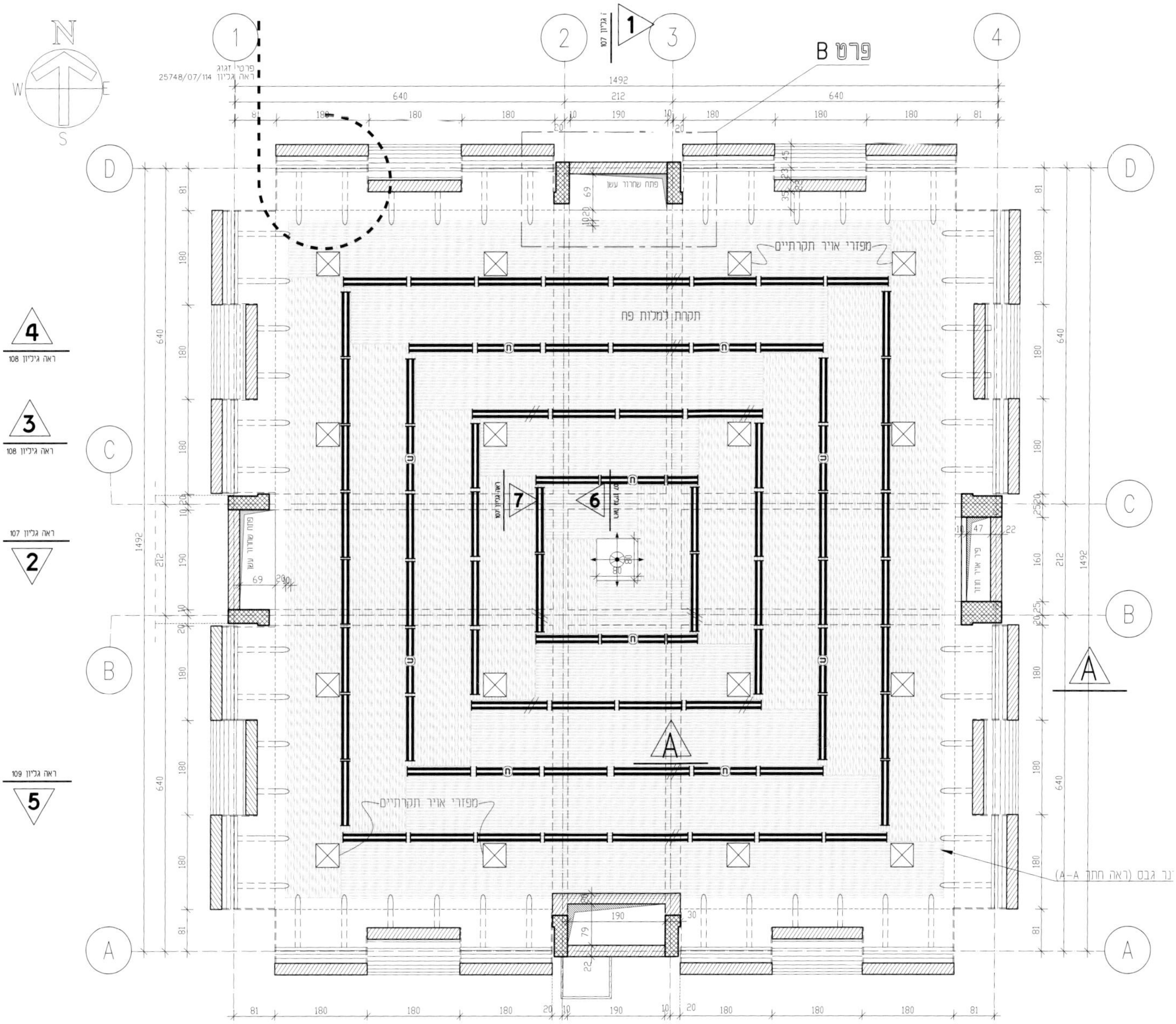

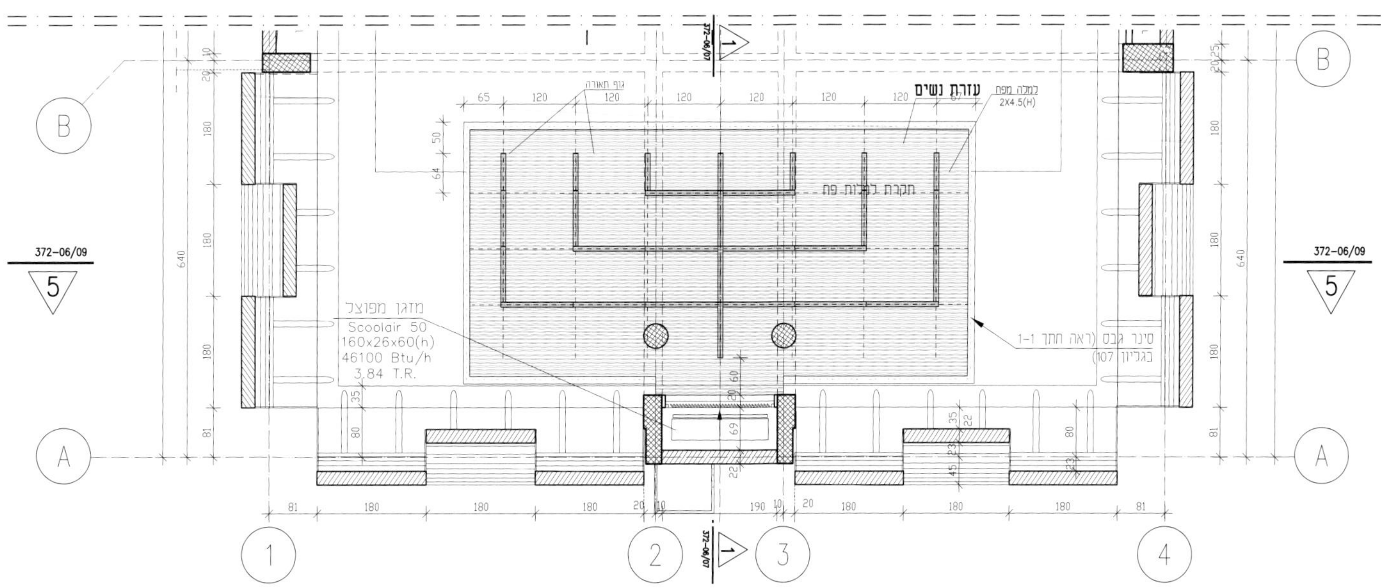

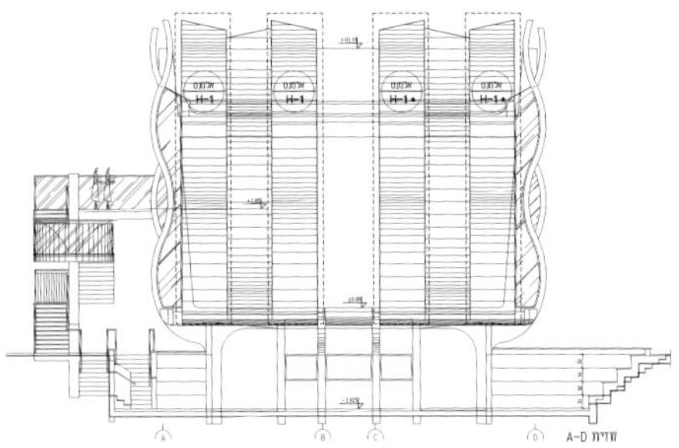

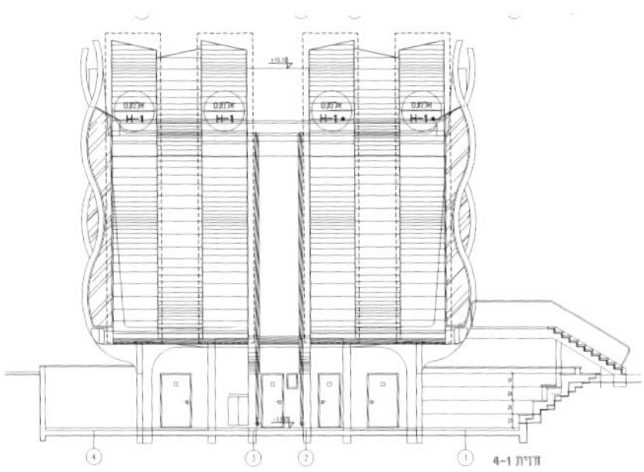

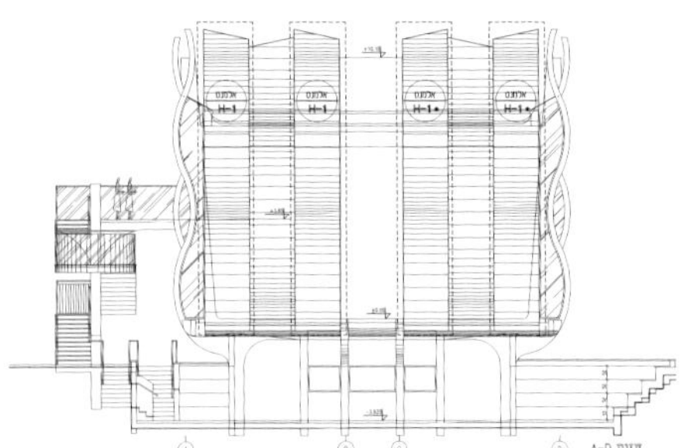

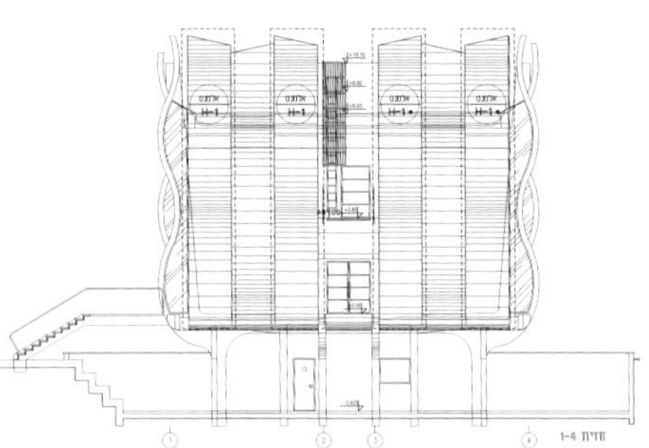

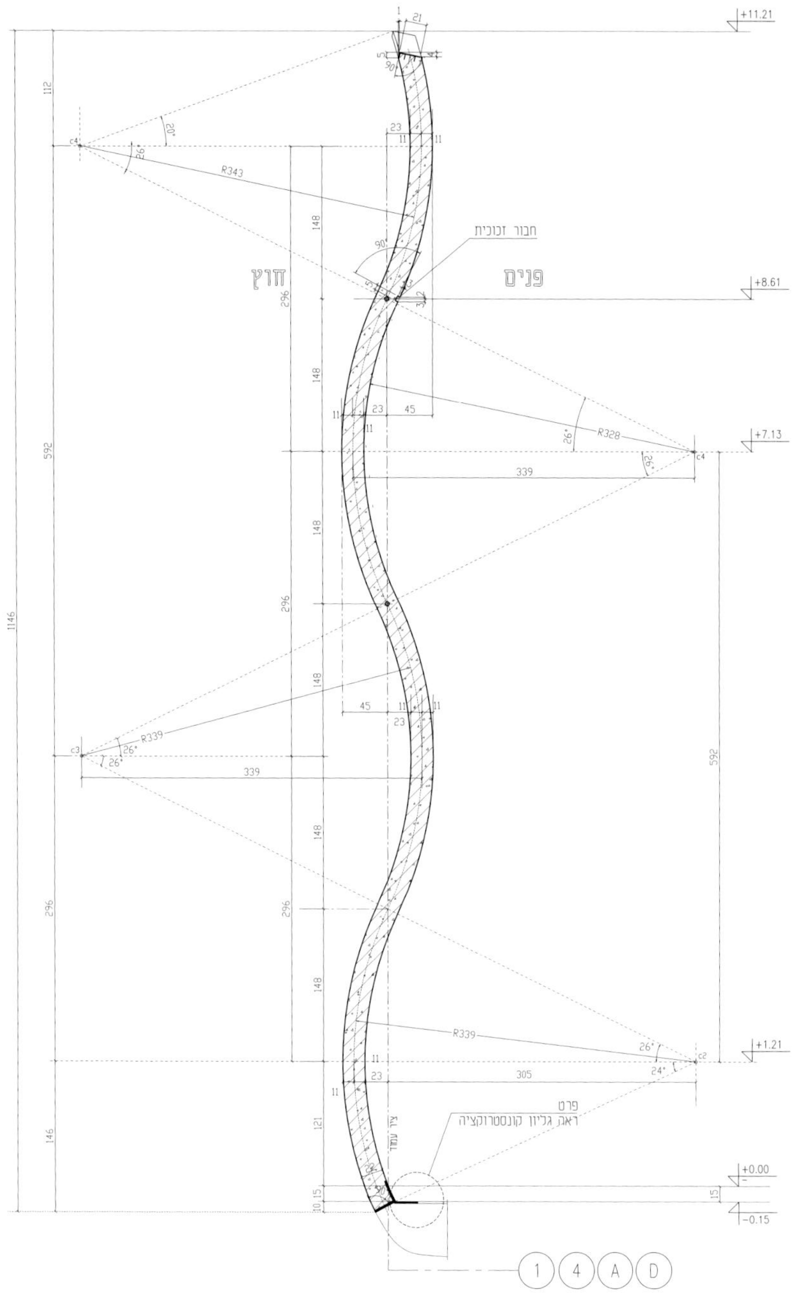

חתך 3-3
ק.מ. 1:25

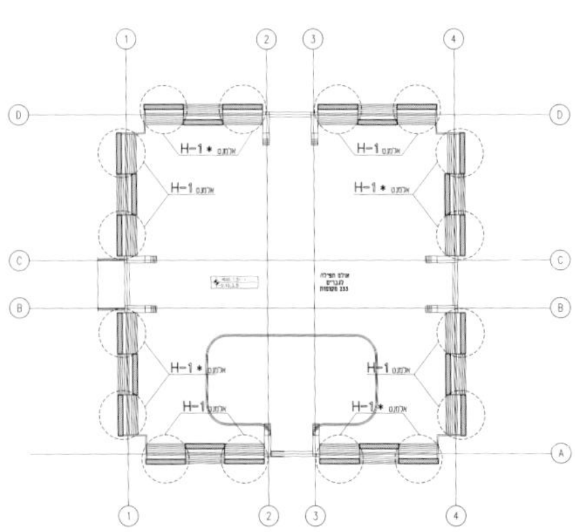

ק.מ. 1:100 סכמה תכנית

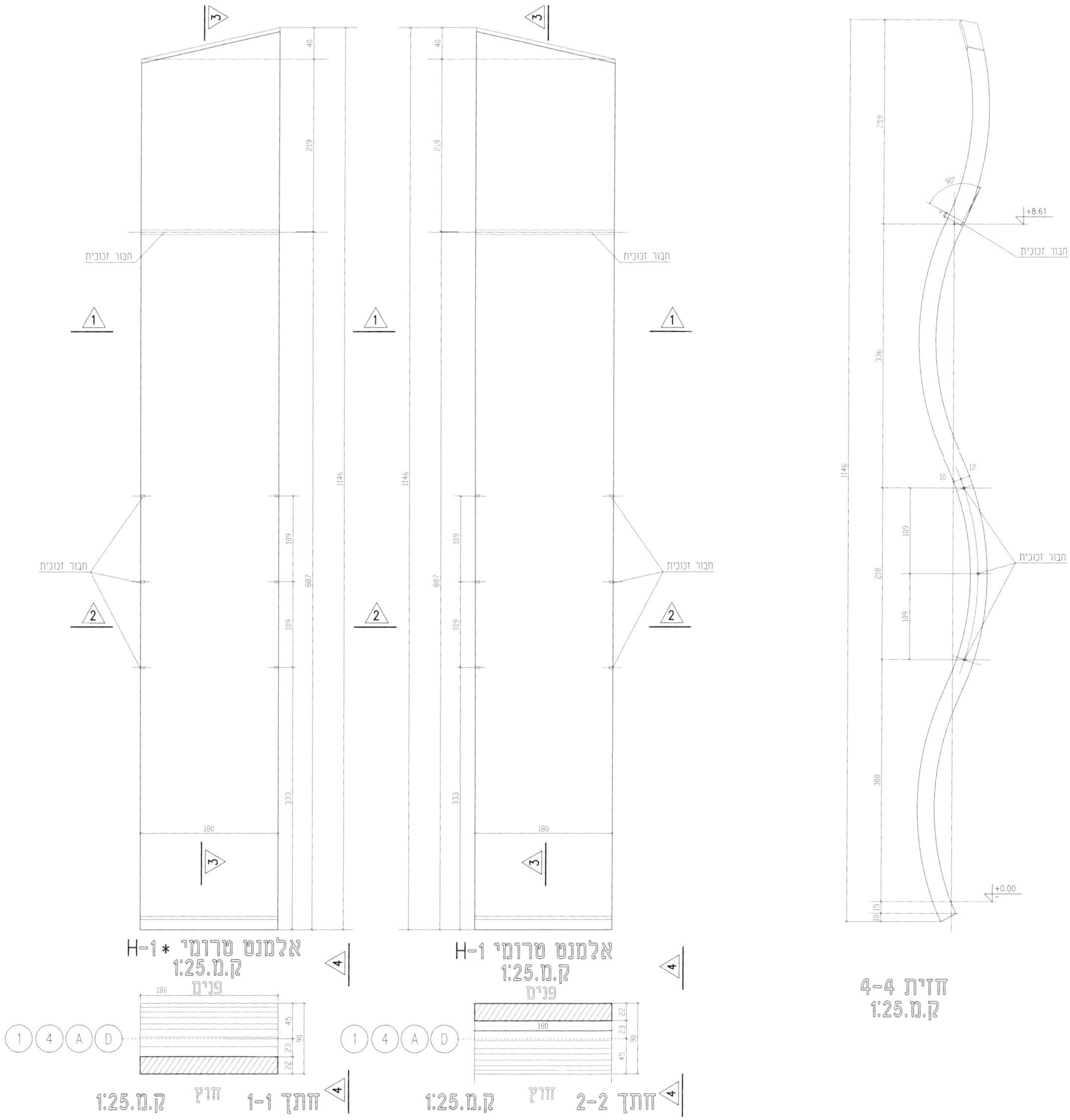
חבור זכוכית
אלמנט טרומי * H-1
ק.מ. 1:25
פנים
חוץ
חתך 1-1
ק.מ. 1:25
אלמנט טרומי H-1
ק.מ. 1:25
פנים
חוץ
חתך 2-2
ק.מ. 1:25
חזית 4-4
ק.מ. 1:25

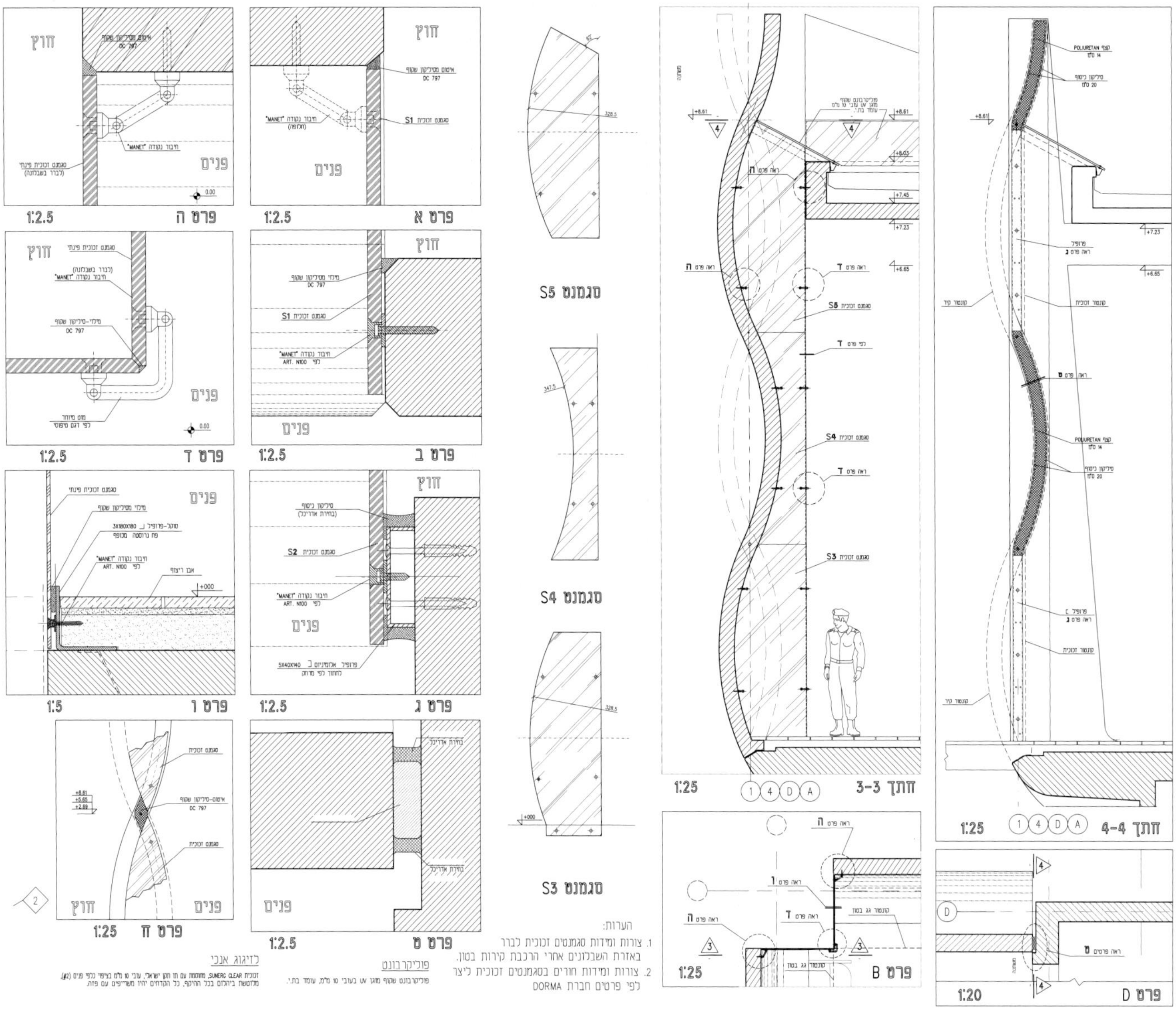
חוץ
פנים
פרט ה 1:2.5
פרט א 1:2.5
פרט ד 1:2.5
פרט ב 1:2.5
פרט ו 1:5
פרט ג 1:2.5
פרט ח 1:25
פרט ט 1:2.5
סגמנט S5
סגמנט S4
סגמנט S3
חתך 3-3 1:25
חתך 4-4 1:25
פרט B 1:25
פרט D 1:20
זיגזג אנכי
פוליקרבונט
הערות:
1. צורות ומידות סגמנטים זכוכית לברר באזרת השבלונים אחרי הרכבת קירות בטון.
2. צורות ומידות חורים בסגמנטים זכוכית ליצר לפי פרטים חברת DORMA

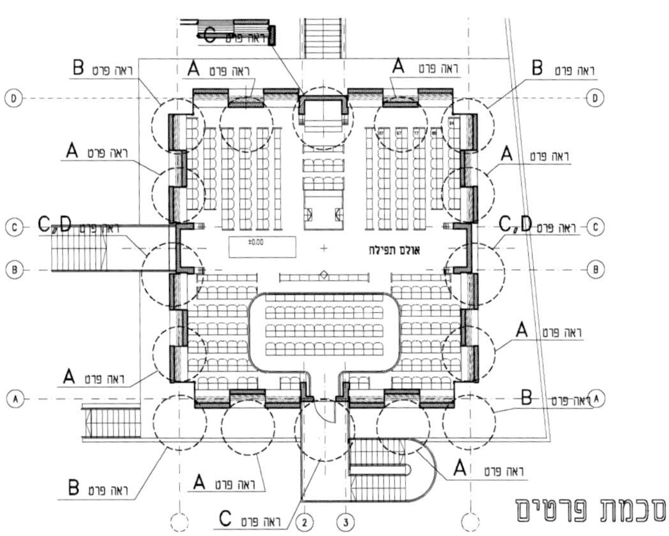
ראה פרט A
ראה פרט B
ראה פרט C
ראה פרט C,D
אולם תפילה
±0.00
סכמת פרטים

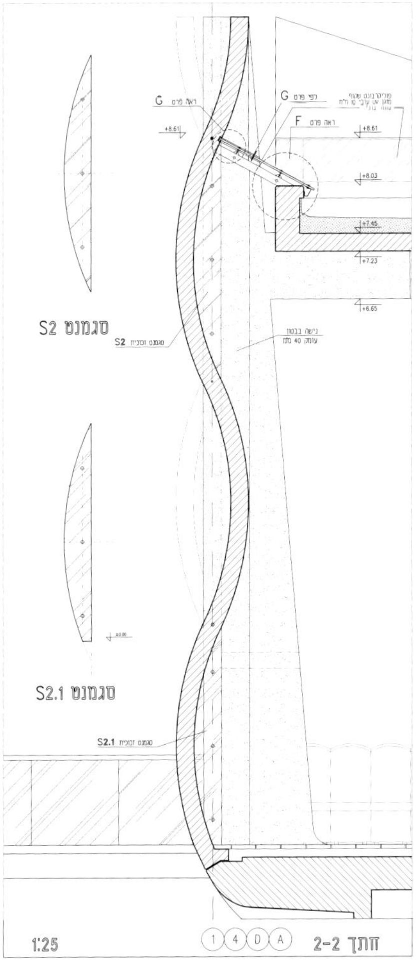

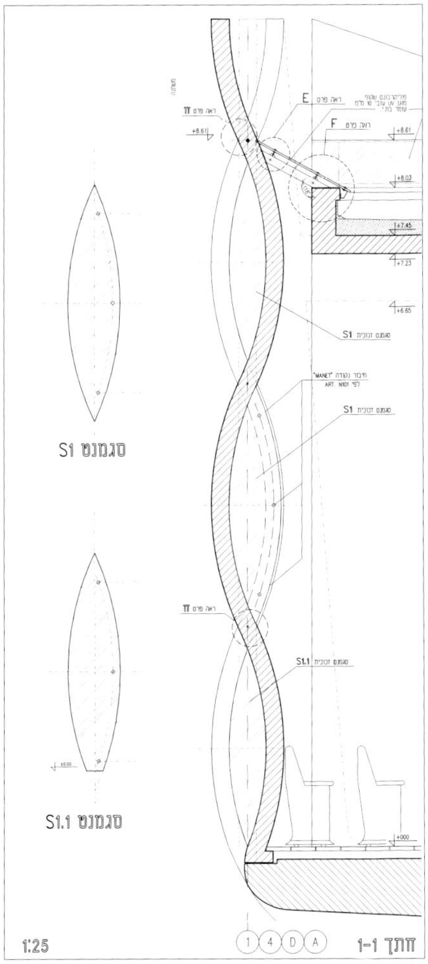

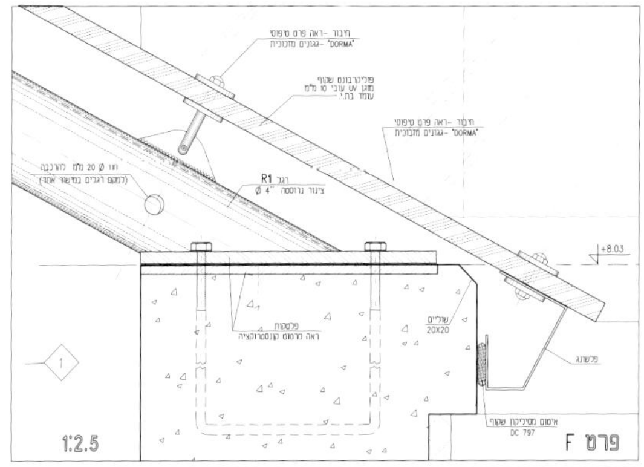

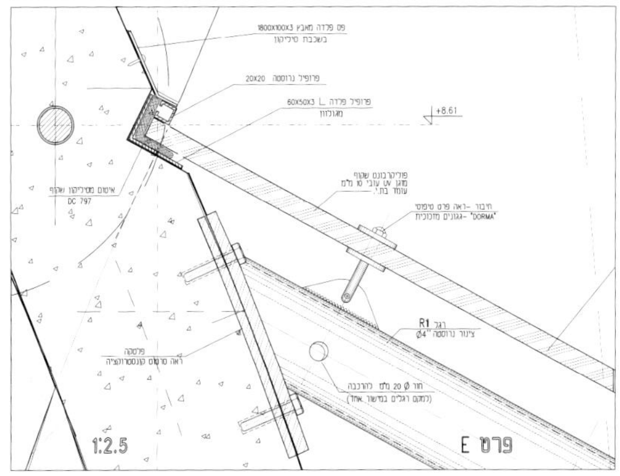

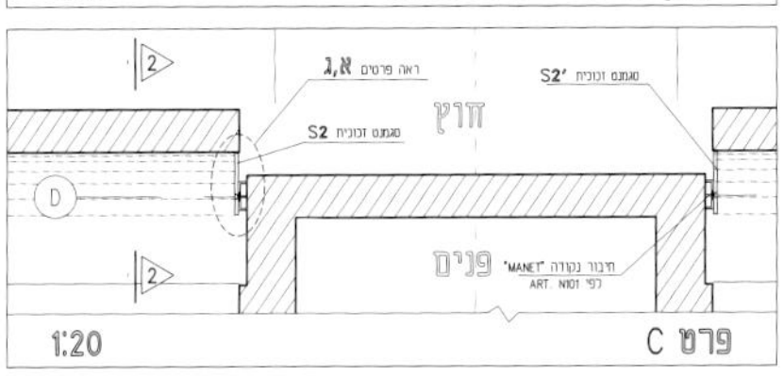

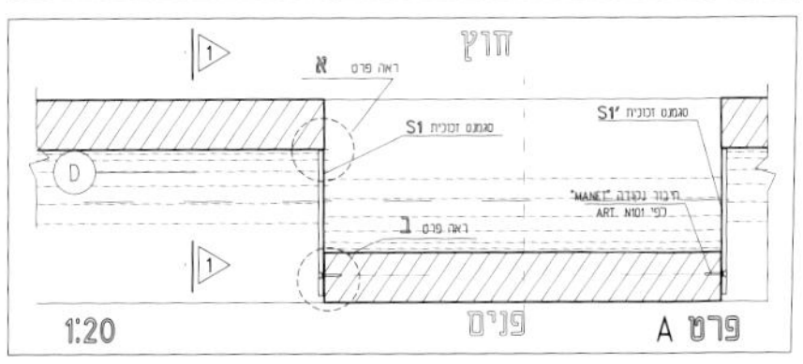

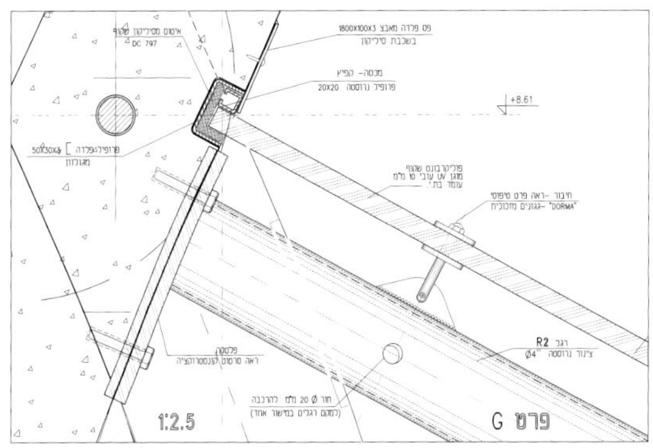

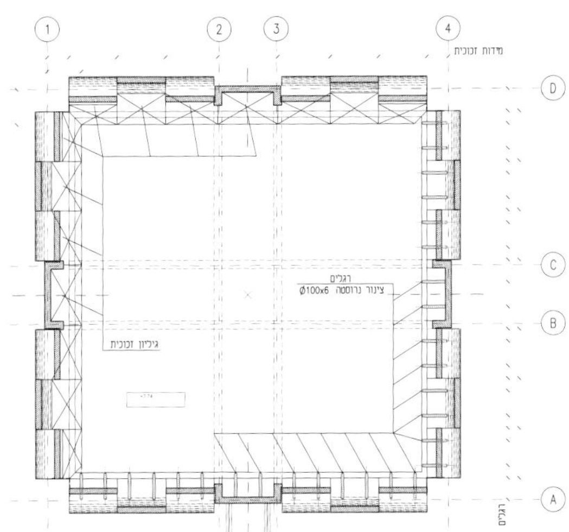

סכמת זיגוג גג מבט מלמעלה 1:100

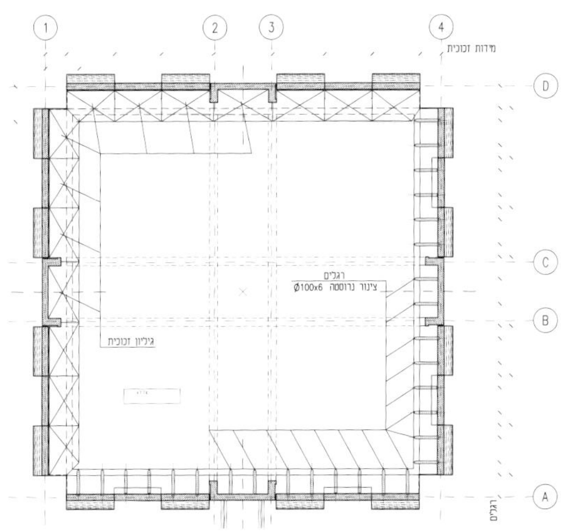

סכמת זיגוג גג חתך 4-4 (במפלס 8.61 +) 1:100

חתך ב -ב 1:25

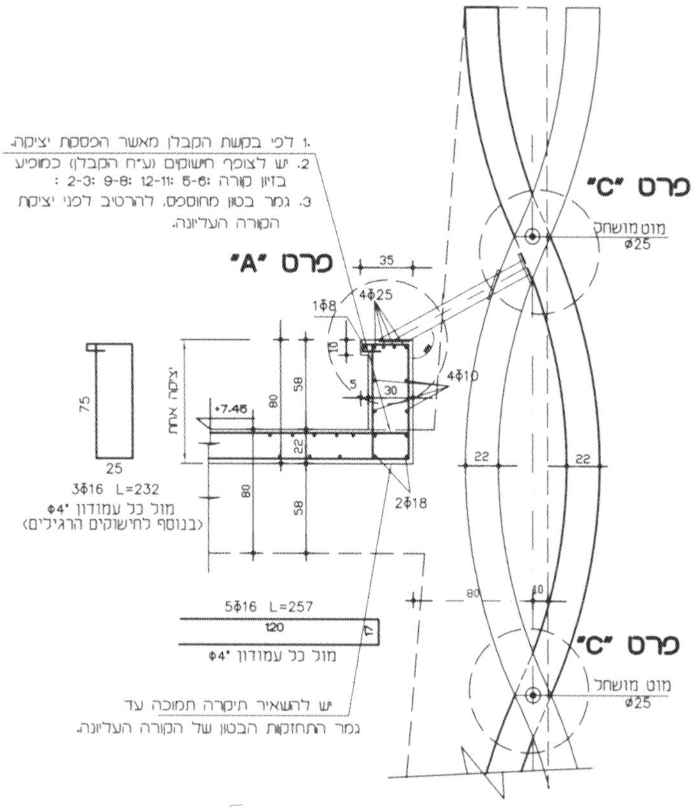

פרט "A" 1:10

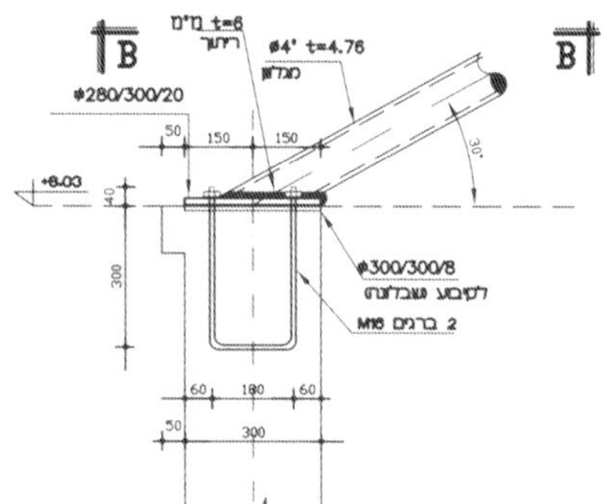

פרט "C1" 1:10
(אלמנט קמור)

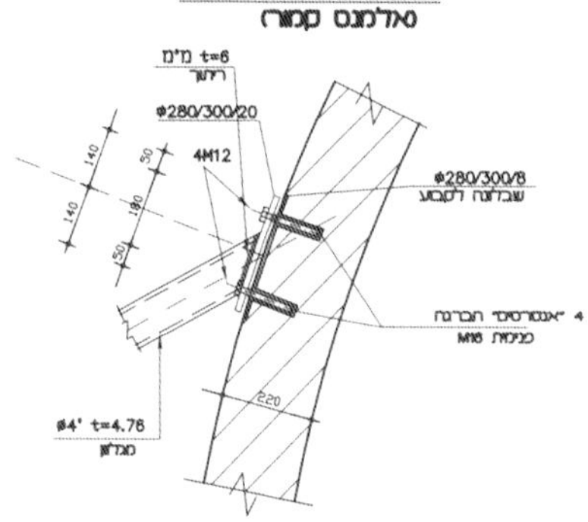

מבט B- B 1:10

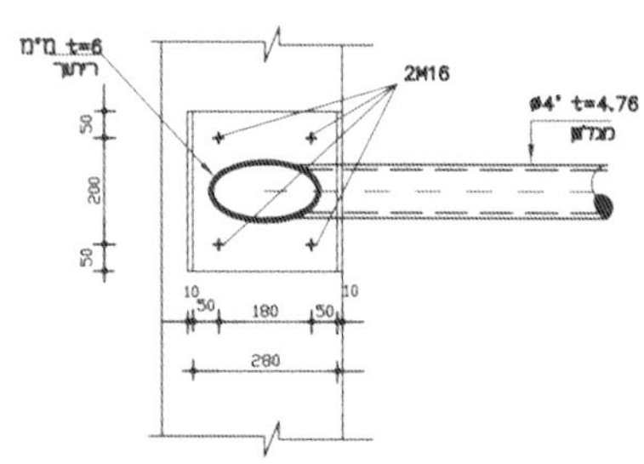

הערה:
כל הברגים יהיו מדרגת חוזק 8.8

פרט "C1" 1:10
(אלמנט קעור)

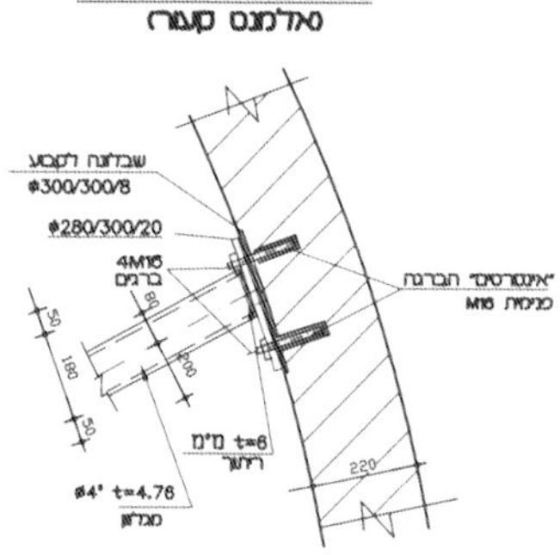

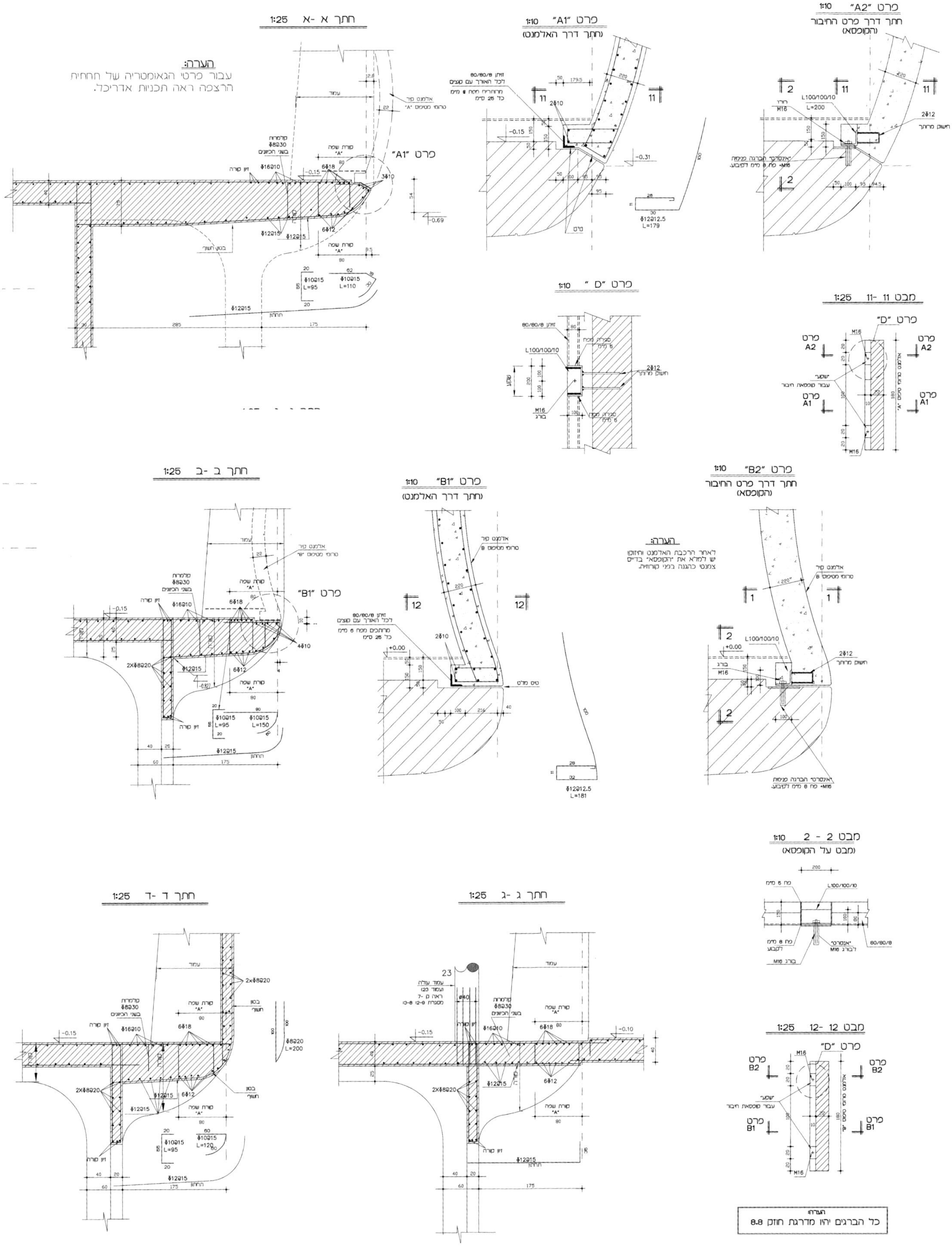

חתך א -א 1:25
הערה:
עבור פרטי הגאומטריה של תחתית הרצפה ראה תכניות אדריכל.
פרט "A1" 1:10
(חתך דרך האלמנט)
פרט "A2" 1:10
חתך דרך פרט החיבור (הקופסא)
פרט "ס" 1:10
מבט 11- 11 1:25
חתך ב -ב 1:25
פרט "B1" 1:10
(חתך דרך האלמנט)
פרט "B2" 1:10
חתך דרך פרט החיבור (הקופסא)
הערה:
לאחר הרכבת האלמנט וחיזוקו יש למלא את "הקופסא" בדייס צמנטי כהגנה בפני קורוזיה.
מבט 2 - 2 1:10
(מבט על הקופסא)
חתך ד -ד 1:25
חתך ג -ג 1:25
מבט 12- 12 1:25
הערה:
כל הברגים יהיו מדרגת חוזק 8.8

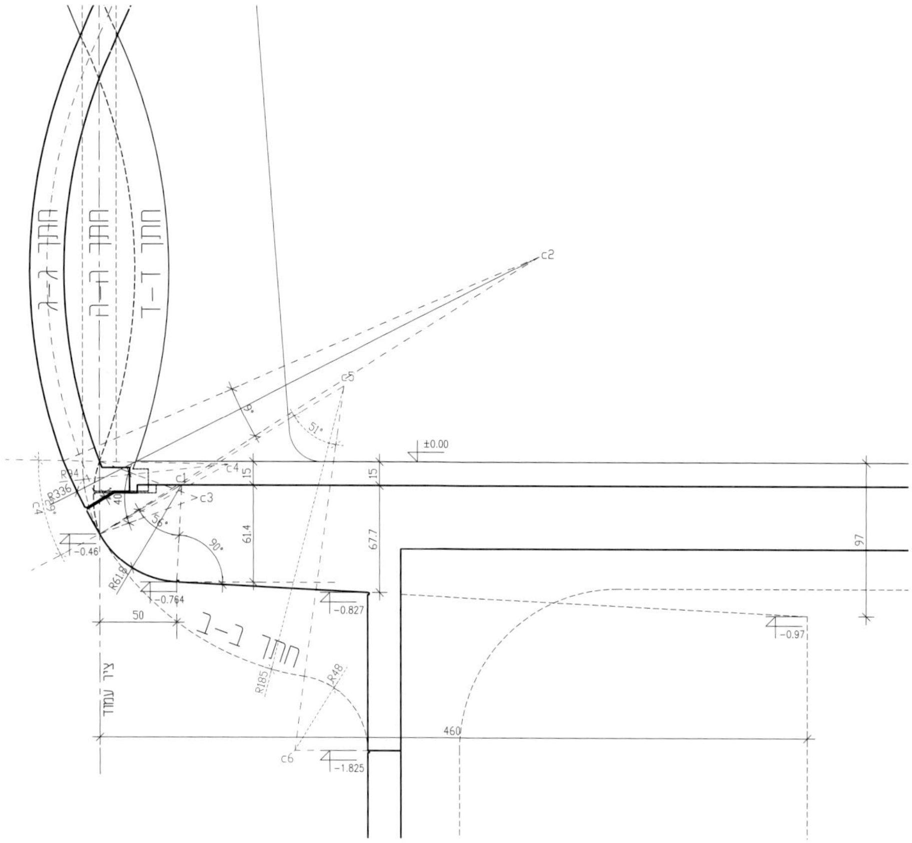

קומפילצית חתכים ב-ב,ג-ג,ד-ד,ה-ה ק.מ. 1:20

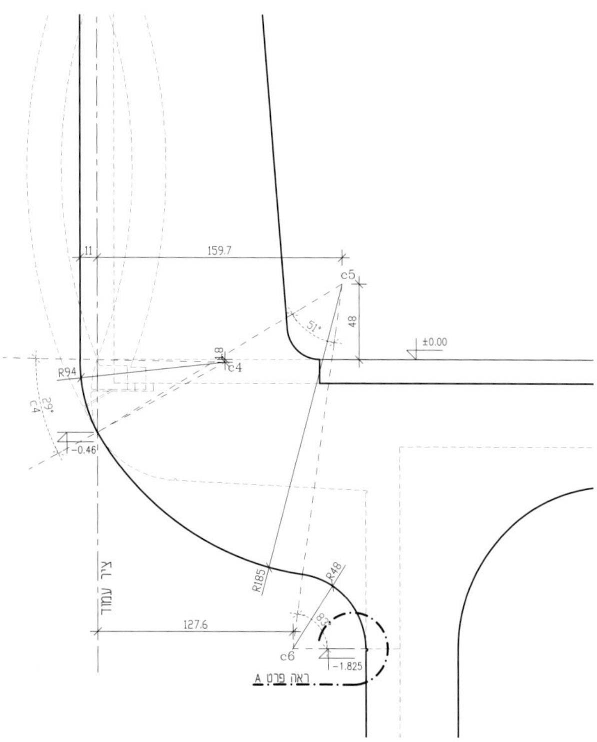

חתך ב-ב ק.מ. 1:20

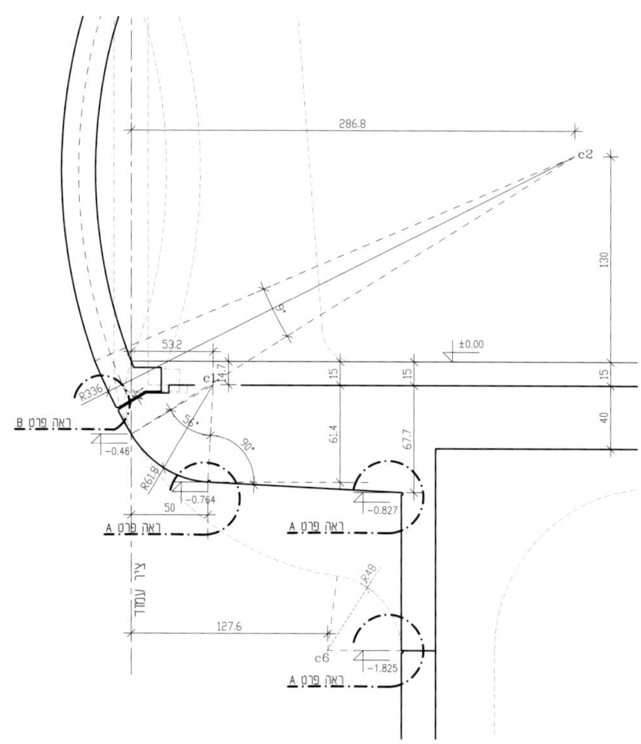

חתך ג-ג ק.מ. 1:20

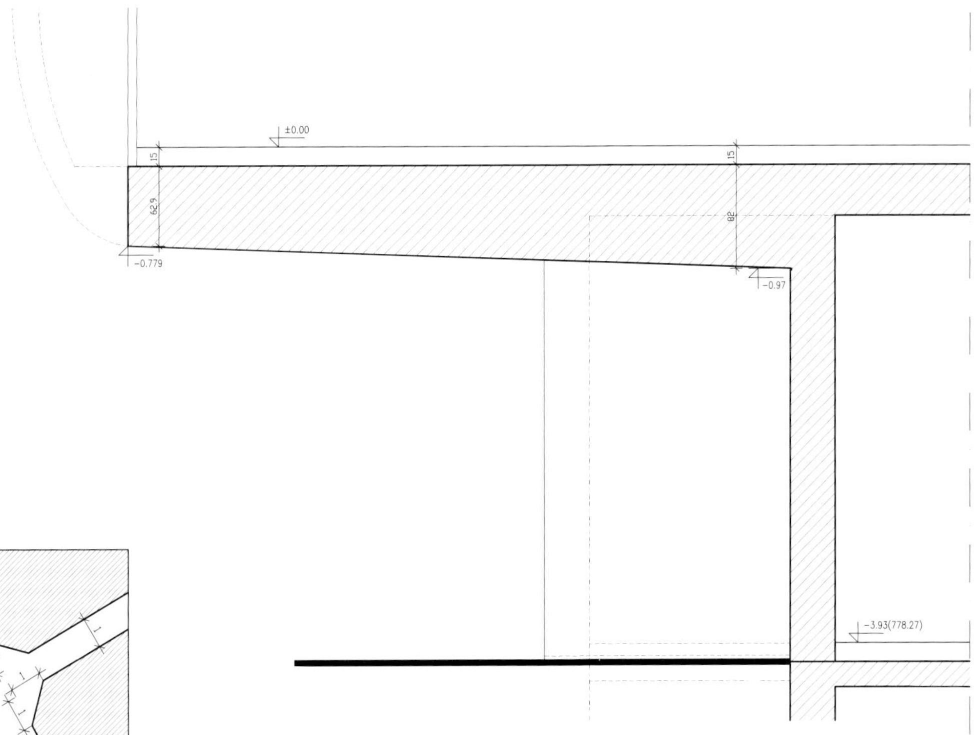

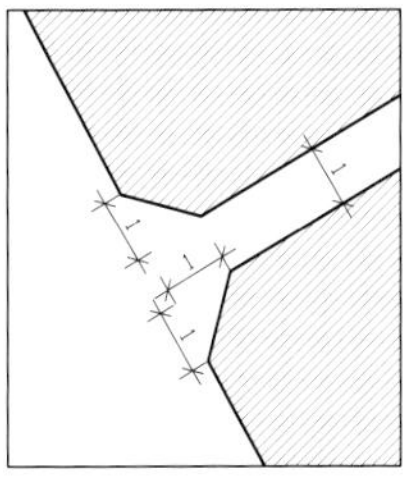

פרט B ק.מ. 1:1
סרגל הפסקת יציקה

חתך א-א ק.מ. 1:25

פרט A ק.מ. 1:1
סרגל הפסקת יציקה

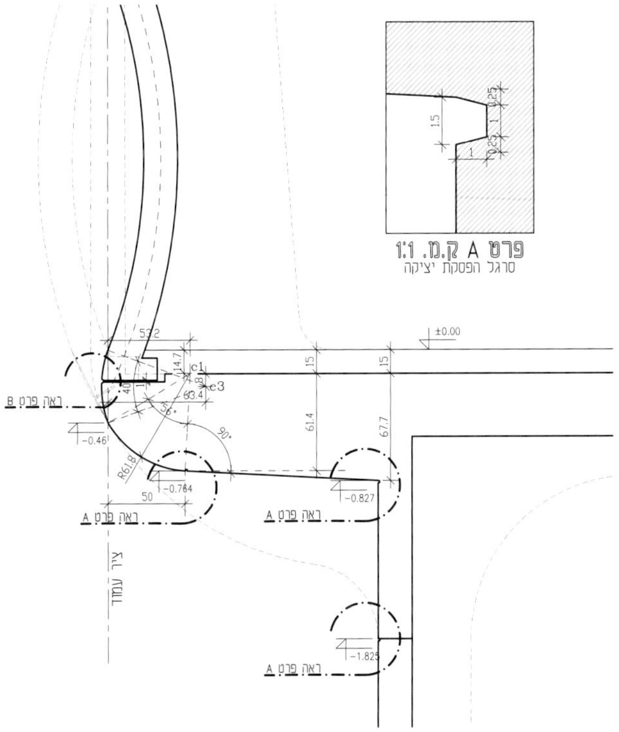

חתך ד-ד ק.מ. 1:20

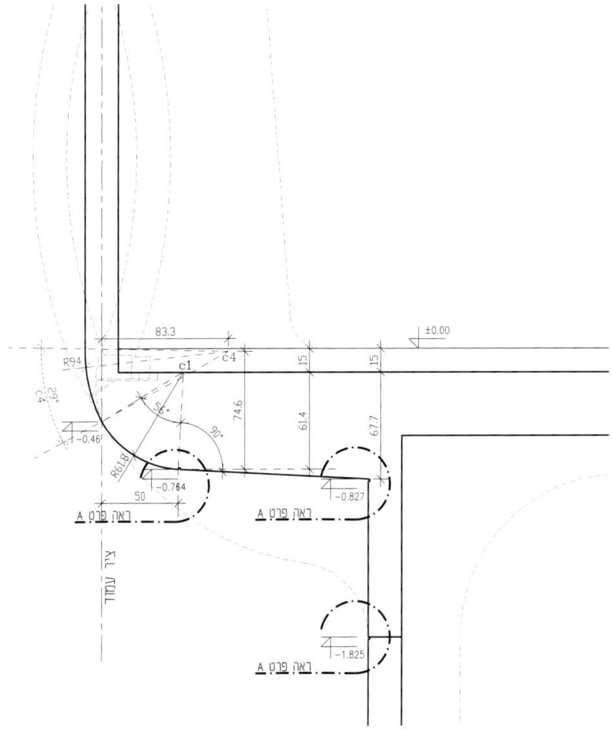

חתך ה-ה ק.מ. 1:20

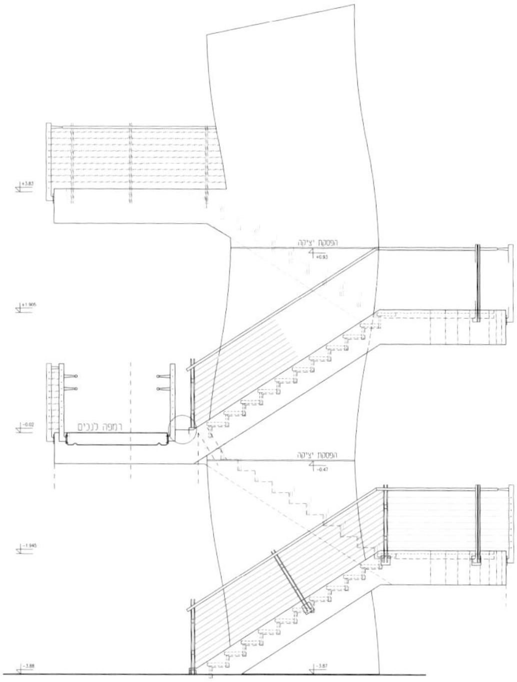

מבט A ק.מ. 1:25

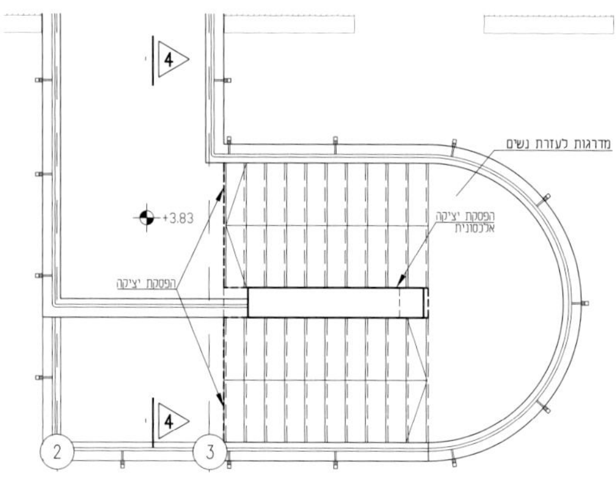

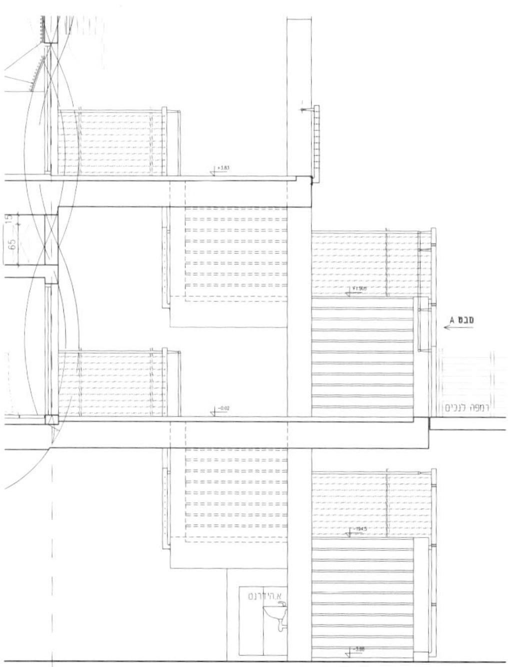

חתך 4-4 ק.מ. 1:25

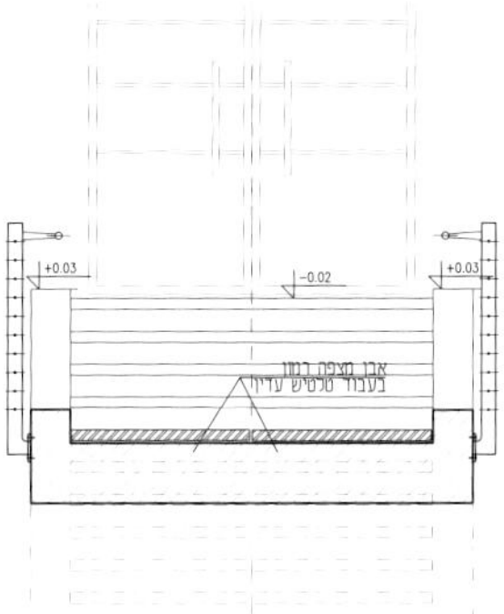

חתך 2-2 ק.מ. 1:25

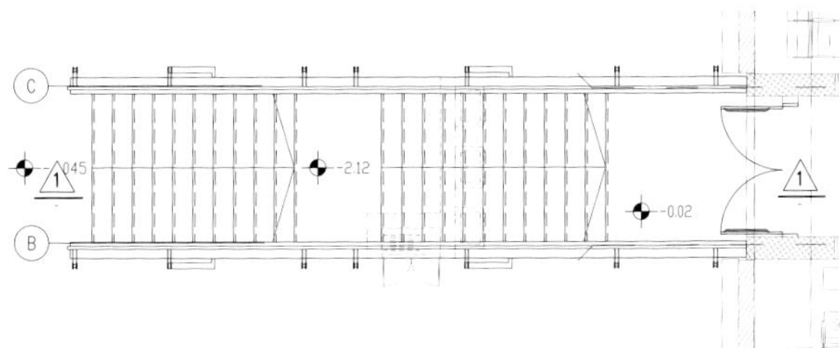

תכנית מדרגות 1 ק.מ. 1:50

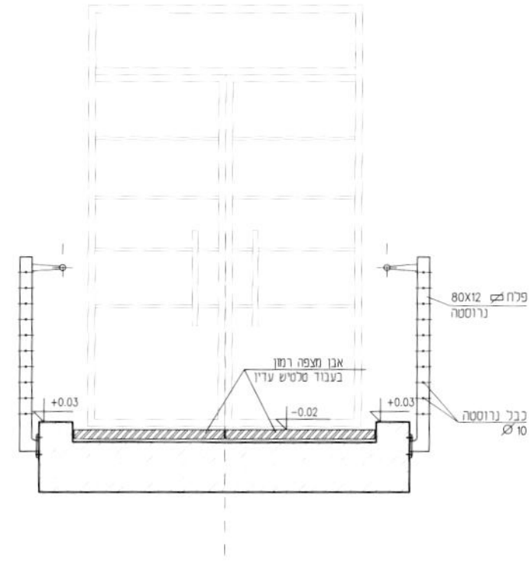

חתך 3-3 ק.מ. 1:25

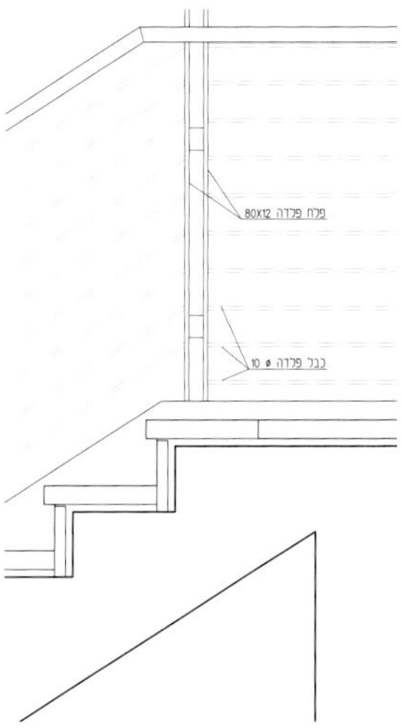

פרט A ק.מ. 1:10

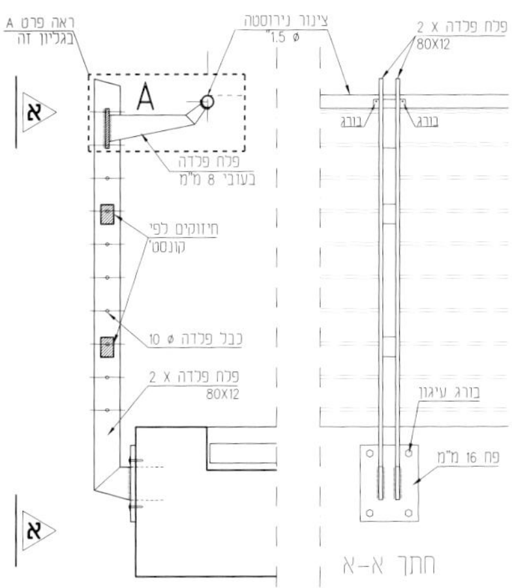

פרט מעקה ק.מ. 1:10

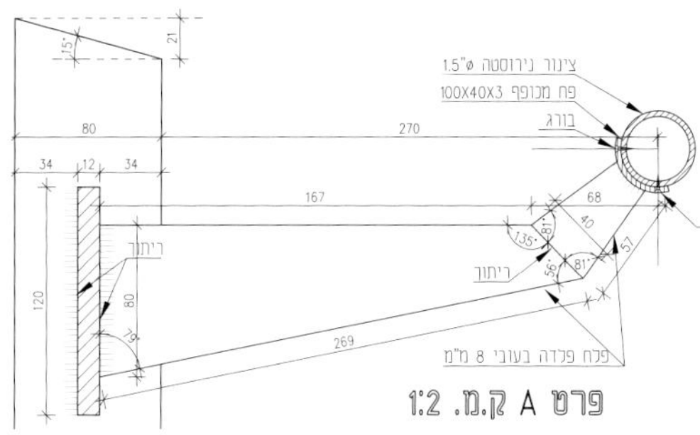

פרט A ק.מ. 1:2

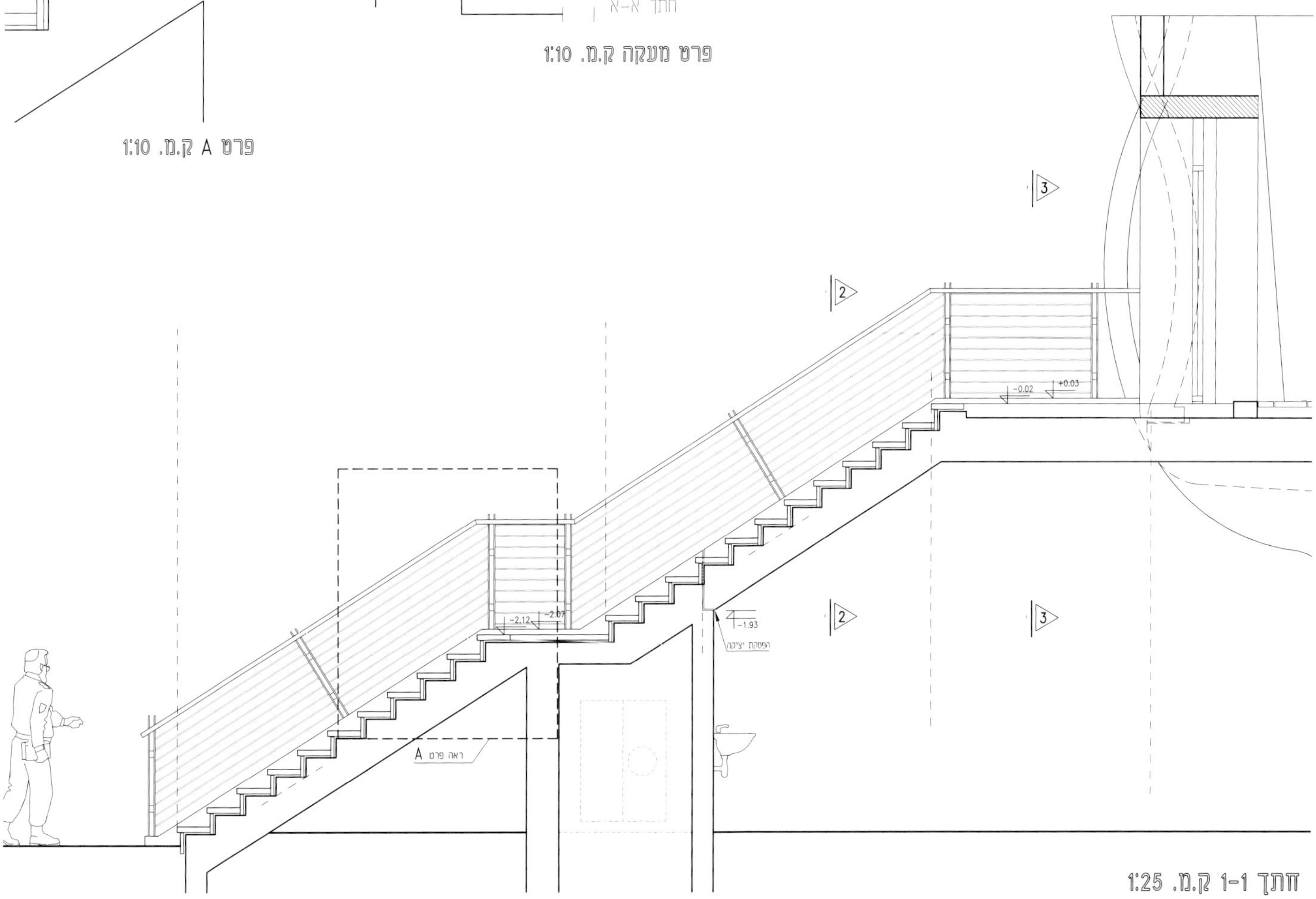

חתך 1-1 ק.מ. 1:25

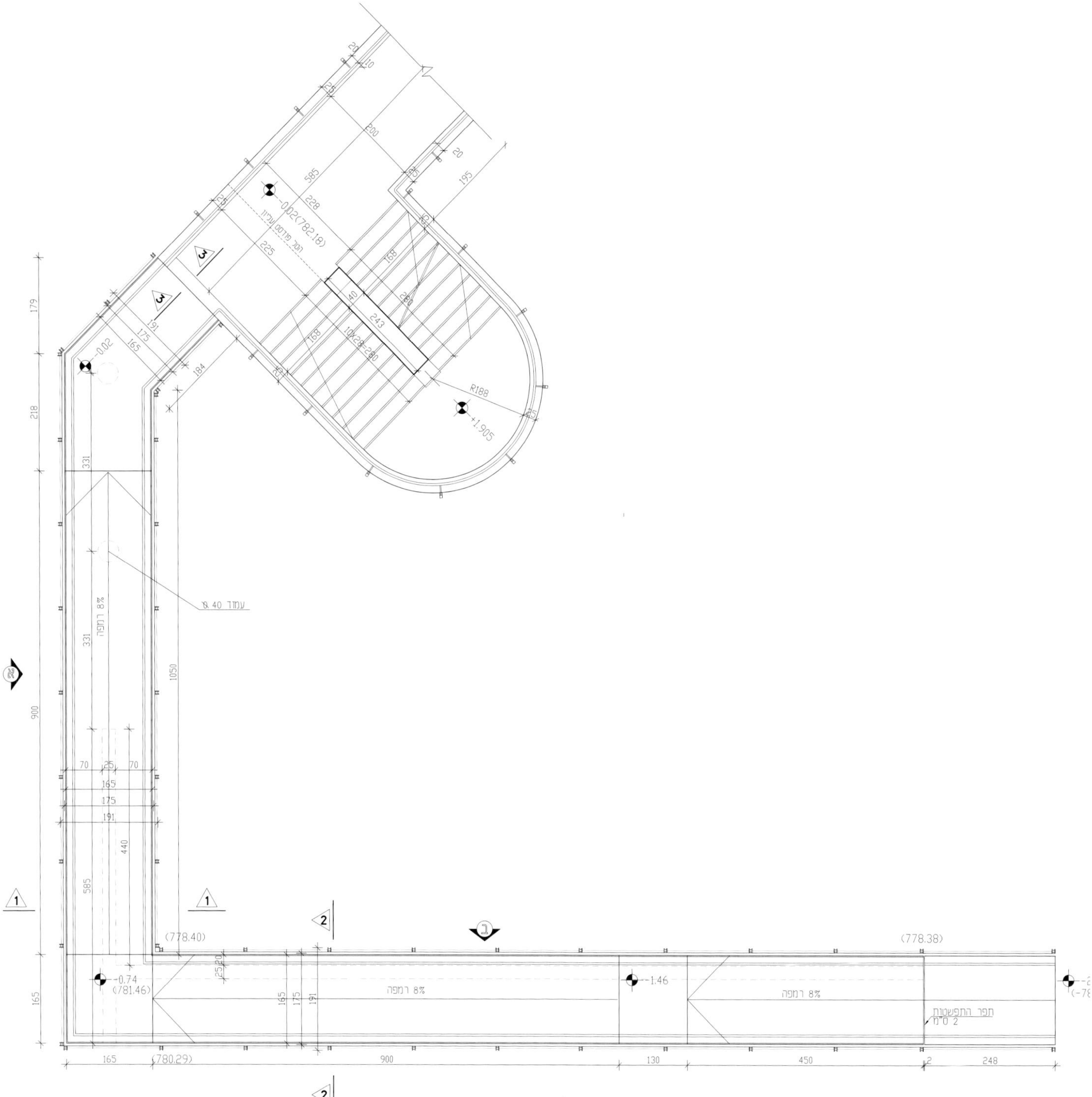

תכנית מעל רמפה ק.מ. 1:50

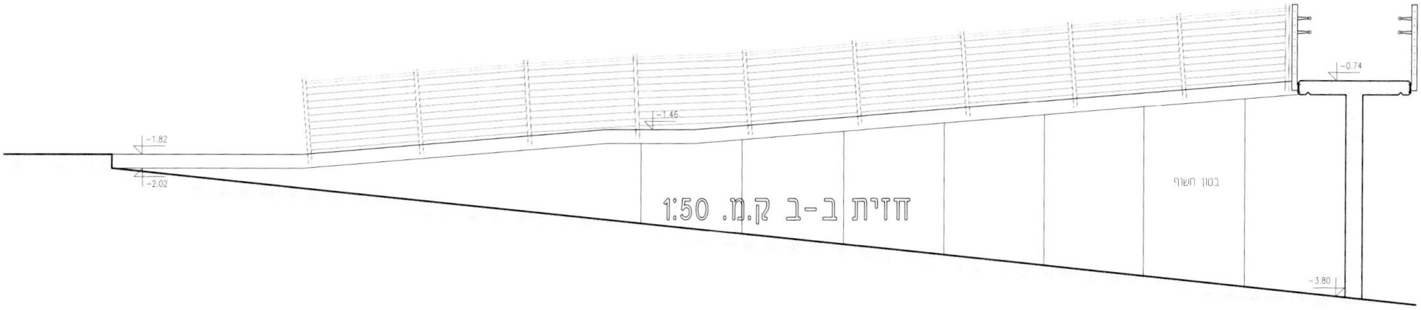

חזית ב-ב ק.מ. 1:50

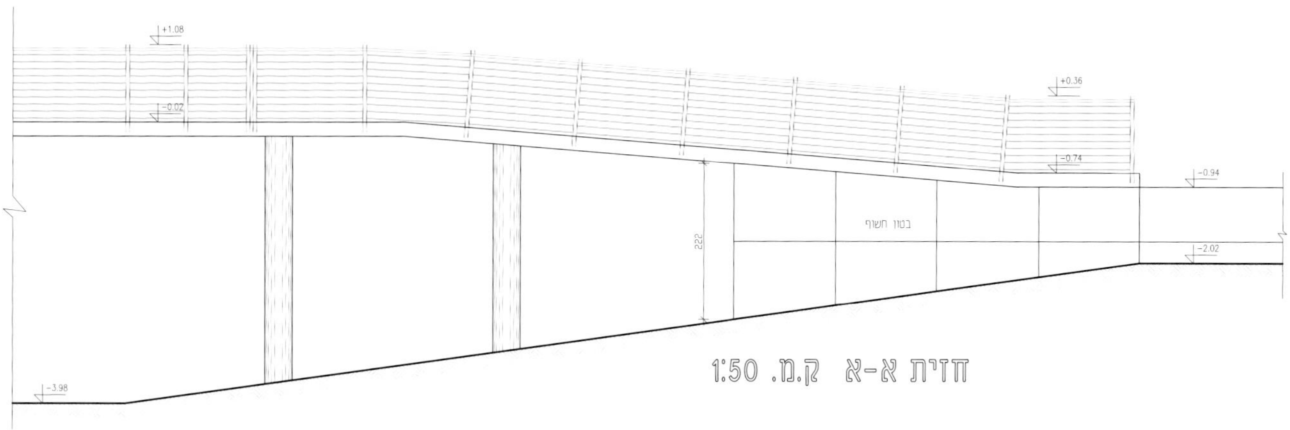

חזית א-א ק.מ. 1:50

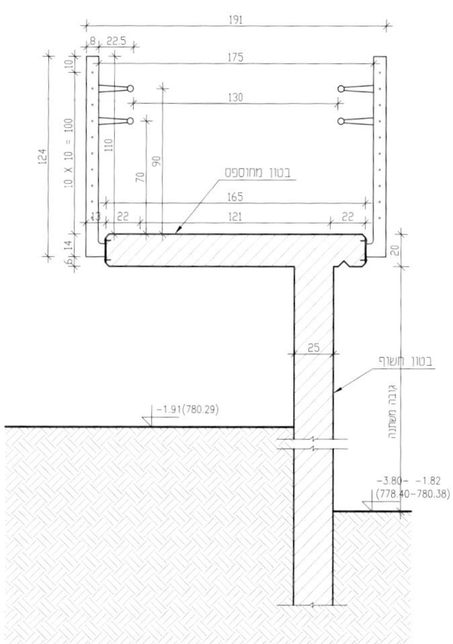

חתך 2-2 ק.מ. 1:25

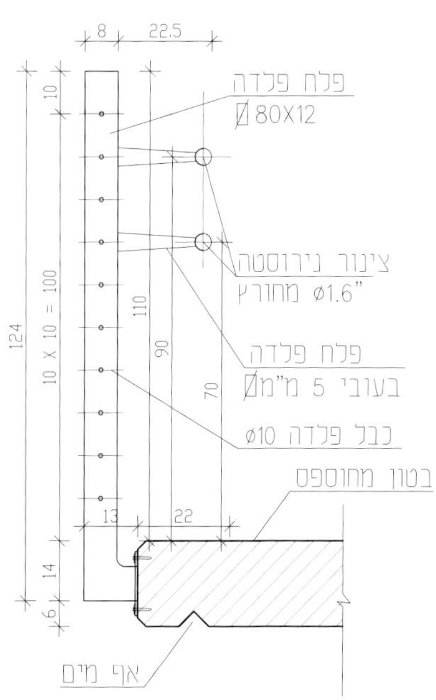

פרט מעקה ק.מ. 1:10

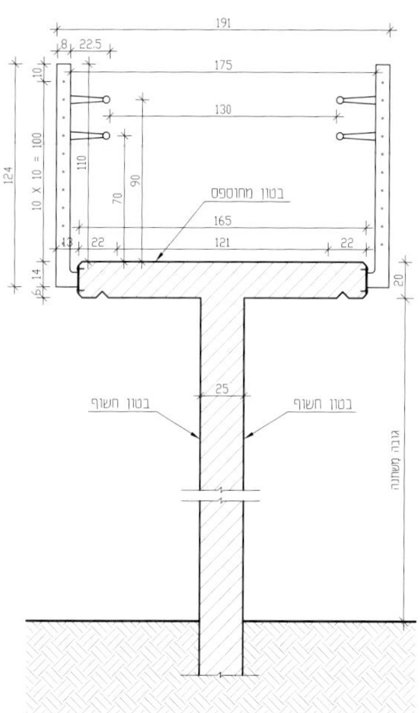

חתך 1-1 ק.מ. 1:25

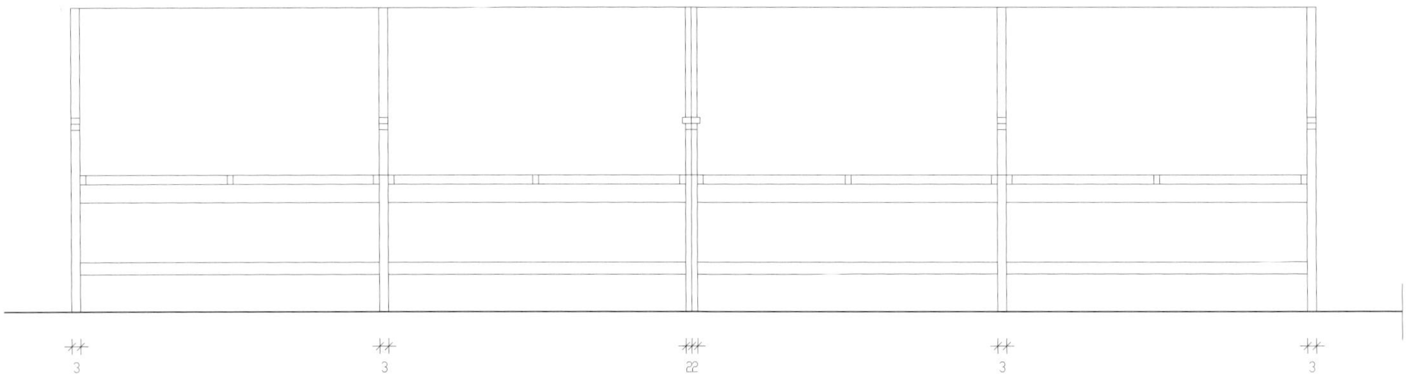

חזית קדמית

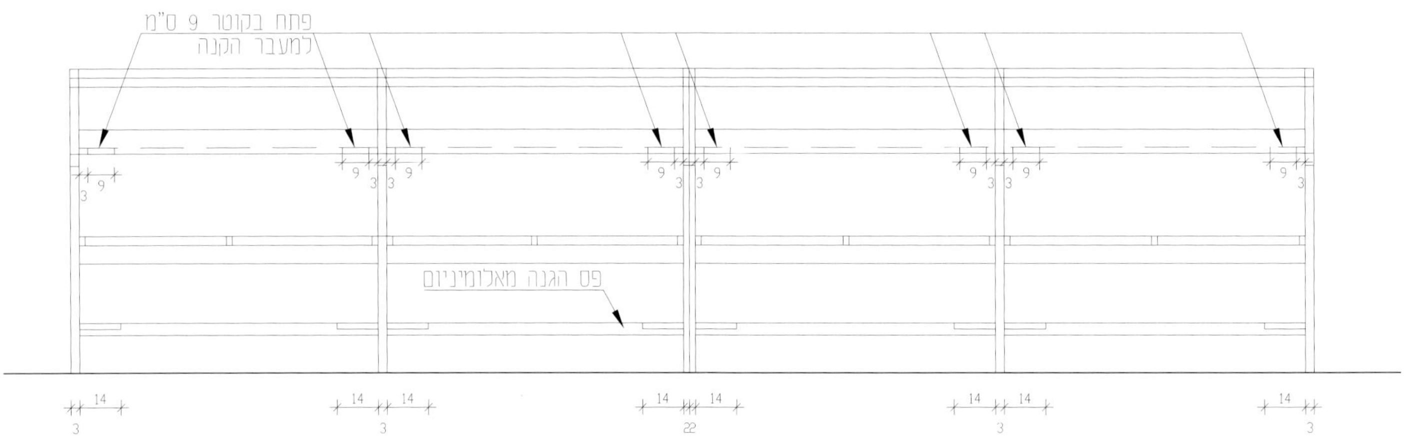

חזית אחורית

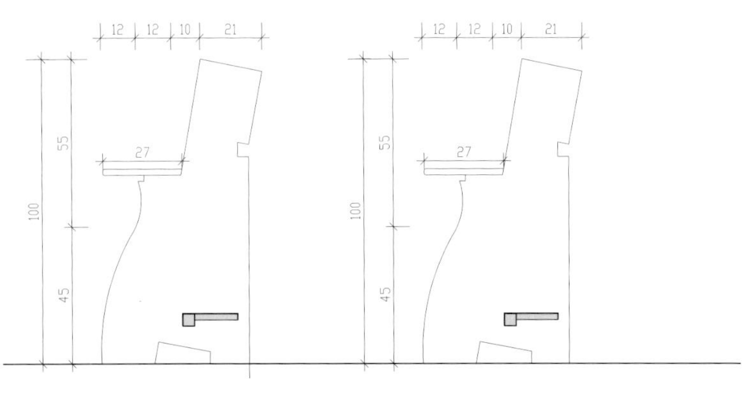

חיזוק בין כל 2 מושבים

חיזוק בין כל 4 מושבים

חיזוקים

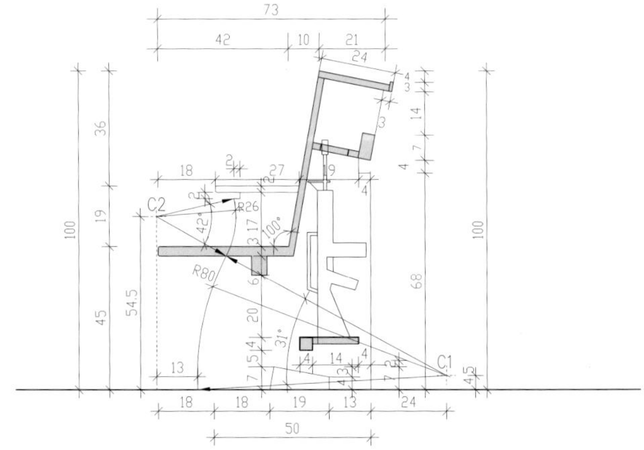

חתך 1 - 1

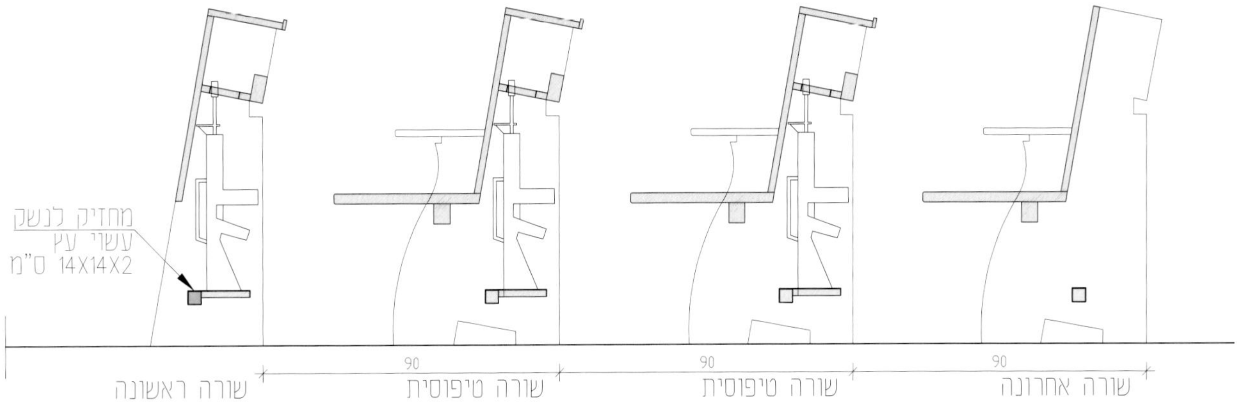

חתך טיפוסי

1

תכנית (קטע טיפוסי)

PROCESS

H-2 W1

תעבורה

תעבורה

תעבורה

THE BUILDING

ESSAY
BY DAVID AMGADI

The Officer's Academy's Synagogue "The Burning Bush"

When you start to write about a building or a large project, it is better if you can disconnect yourself from individual systems of priorities and examine the "architectural object" from a truly objective perspective. This of course is almost impossible to do. Writing brings an author's personal past and priorities, and they influence their judgment, as evident in The Burning Bush Synagogue in the officer's academy. It is hard to disconnect your identity, even if you are not religious by conventional standards. The site is an Israeli "junction." Thousands of young people from all corners of the population pass through it every year. The aura emitting from "modest sanctuary" from the building is immense. The synagogue's location is related to two biblical stories. To Moses, a prophet and leader, who undertook his destiny through revelation at the burning bush; and to the story of the judge Gideon, who became a leader and courageous warrior. God's revelation and his undertaking of his destiny had the presence of fire, which engulfed all that was offered. From the many responses voiced by cadets who served in the academy and successfully passed their officer's training, it is clear they remember their visit to the synagogue as an uplifting experience.

A religious building can offer a simple image of familiar context and stories along with architectural commentary that is not necessarily "sophisticated." And it can be complex with interpretation that requires clarifications and searching.

The Burning Bush Synagogue was planned as a simple symmetric building. One which sits on an elevated box made of exposed concrete. One of the most important rules of classicism is symmetry. Is there a reason that all sides of the building (the box) must be identical? Symmetry represents the stationary, remaining passive and a lack of democracy. Asymmetric objects are considered live organisms, free from binding conventions and rules. Like music. For example, the dissonance present in the music of Arnold Schoenberg conveys freedom and release. Modern physics has also found what has been actually defined as the "God Particle" (Higgs boson) – and it is an asymmetrical product.

Nevertheless, symmetry provides us harmony, quiet, stability and a feeling of "being balanced." In nature, there are animals that research has shown to be attracted to symmetric objects, mainly because they are easy to identify in a noisy and bustling environment.

The following churches are considered icons and religious structures representing architectural splendor. The religious and cultural experience they provide is nothing less than significant:

Cathedral Rotterdam – Paris – bilateral symmetry (Bishop Maurice de Sully and others);

DAVID AMGADI, born in Teheran in 1957, is the Head of the Planning Department at the ILA (Israel Lands Authority). At this institution, he is responsible for the initiation, direction and guidance of structure plans, development plans and detailed town plans as well as development programs at all levels. David is a regular speaker on town planning issues at various local and international forums. He holds a Bachelor of Architecture and Town Planning from The Technion - Israel Institute of Technology, a public research University in Haifa, Israel.

Chapelle Ronchamp – clear asymmetry (Le Corbusier).

Naturally, it is the final result that can be judged. The idea behind the building, and its connection to the story can almost be heard – the time and location the moment was born. The relationship between the interior and exterior, from all aspects – the penetration of natural light, quality of space, level of completion, but mainly from the spiritual experience rooted in the visitor's memories and culture, is almost tangible.

The same is true for the Burning Bush. The meeting between straight lines and flowing waves made of exposed concrete, a contradiction between the hard and solid, and the soft roundness flowing endlessly upwards. We can imagine the continuation of the wave (the flame) ever upwards. The light penetrating from above and from all sides, open corners with no clear divider with the outside, transparency, and a plethora of reappearing and changing shapes. This transparency between the inside and out that stands out in daytime, erupts in the twilight hours, when the flame can be seen from a distance as a vibrant ember emitting light and warmth, while enforcing the image of the biblical story.

The entrance used to access the sanctuary presents steps that must be taken to reach the "place" (physically and spiritually). The physical ascent also represents the spiritual ascent. The steps are few and lead into the "fire" – the familiar biblical story of experimenting with material that can withstand fire.

The interior design is warm, simple and familiar – wood. The sitting system is in the spirit of the "book and the sword" – soldiers arrive with their weapons (the sword) and place them conveniently in the place modeled in the furniture, immediately below their prayer books, allowing them the solitude they desire without ever distancing themselves from their tools of battle.

The soldier is next to his weapon even when in prayer. The design is related to Gideon's choosing his soldiers when stopping to drink. Those who remained with their weapons (according to one commentary), even when partaking of the river's waters, were chosen. They joined the ranks to conquer the Midianites, and the others were sent back to their homes.

The Burning Bush Synagogue leaves a religious impression on the observer and joins other iconic sites that are part of the Israeli architectural experience and allows us to define the local construction of future religious buildings.

—David Amgadi
Tel Aviv, Israel February 2020

"...ממני תראו וכן תעשו"

מבנה זה
תוכנן ע״י
ארמון
אדריכלים
ט״ז בחשון תש״ע • 3 בנובמבר 2009

"..והנה הסנה בוער באש
והסנה איננו אפל.."
(שמות פרק ג' פסוק ב')

"..והנה הסנה בוער באש
והסנה איננו אכל.."
(שמות פרק ג׳ פסוק ב׳)

"..והנה הסנה בוער באש
והסנה איננו אכל.."
(שמות פרק ג' פסוק ב')

JNF. For ISRAEL Forever.
Ruderman Family
This Synagogue is dedicated by The
Ruderman Family Foundation
in memory of our beloved parents
and grandparents
Jacob and Rose
Ruderman
Max and Freda
Jortner
May their memories be a blessing
and inspiration to all those
who fight for Israel's freedom.
november 2009
חשון תש"ע

יציאה

יציאה

יציאה

"הסייף והספר
ירדו כרוכים מן השמים"
מדרש רבה, ד׳ ב׳

יציאה

"..והנה הסנה בוער באש
והסנה איננו אכל.."

OPENING CEREMONY

Gabi Ashkenazi, Israel Defense Forces Chief of Staff at the time of the Opening Ceremony with Shira and Jay Ruderman, Executive Director and President of the Ruderman Family Foundation. the main sponsors for the construction of the Burning Bush Synagogue project, during the opening ceremony held on November 3, 2009. (Opposite page top and middle). Working to promote strategic philanthropy in Israel, the United States and around the world, The Ruderman Family Foundation is a professional entity engaging in action in the field of leading strategic processes with far-reaching impact. The Institution holds the beief that charitable funds have a significant role in leading complex and multi-systemic social processes.

Gabi Ashkenazi and Eliezer Armon during the opening ceremony. Dignitaries at the prestigious inauguration ceremony also included the Minister of Defense, Knesseth Member Matan Vilnai, distinguished additional donors, commanders and soldiers at the base. (Opposite page bottom left). Eliezer Armon entering the Torah book into the synagogue during the early stages of the ceremony. (Opposite page far right)

Shira (on the right) and Jay (on the left) Ruderman, Of the Ruderman fund, the contributors of the synagogue, together with Gabi Ashkenazi (up) IDF chief of staff at the time (above). Architect Eliezer Armon together with, Gabi Ashkenazi, IDF chief of staff at the time (bottom left).

INTERVIEW

WITH ELI ARMON CONDUCTED BY VLADIMIR BELOGOLOVSKY

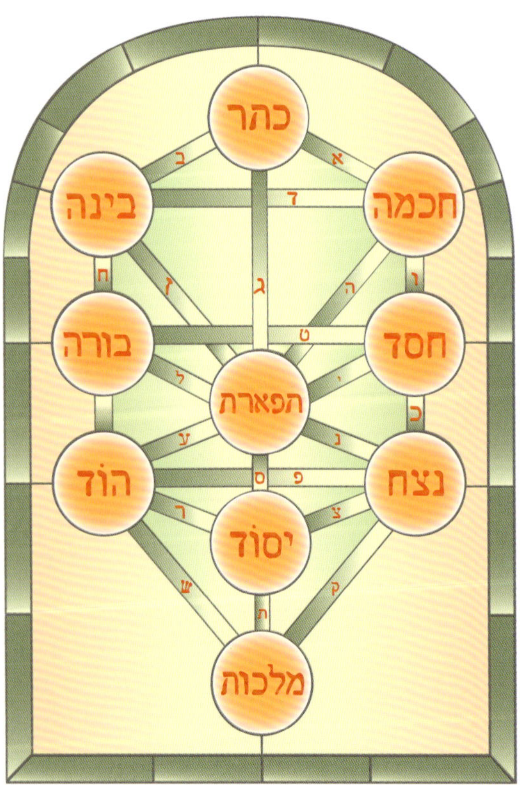

The 10 spheres of Kabbalah

"It Is a Divine Feeling When You Can Leave the First Mark on the Ground" In conversation with Eliezer Armon of Armon Architects & Town Planners. December 19, 2019. By Vladimir Belogolovsky

Eli Armon was born in Tel Aviv, Israel in 1955. He tried a number of career choices before, at the age of 25, pursuing yet another undertaking, a prospect of becoming an architect. First, he acquired an engineering technician degree in high school, then served three and a half years in the Israeli Defense Forces, and after years of duty in reserve he was discharged with the rank of Lieutenant Colonel. Furthermore, he studied physics and mathematics, albeit for just one semester at Tel Aviv University. It was Armon's love for engineering, physics, mathematics, history, art, and the capacity to perceive complex spatial relationships that he felt could provide him the right foundation for another interest that eventually has become his life-long passion – architecture. He gave it a try. It was the assurance of both graphologist and palm reader at the time that affirmed his decision. Along the way, he also dedicated himself to becoming a Kabbalah scholar and a martial artist, and after 50 years of practice he is a 7th Dan master in Dennis survival Jiu-Jitsu method. Both fascinations have contributed profoundly to his work as an architect.

After graduating from the Architecture School at the Technion in Haifa in 1985, Armon started his own practice, but immediately realized that he still lacked professional experience. He then worked at a large office in Tel Aviv and soon was hired as the chief engineer of Immanuel, a small settlement in Samaria. That job prepared him well for another opportunity that came a few years later when he was hired as the chief engineer of Be'er Sheva, the capital of the Negev and the largest city in the south of Israel. To take that job he relocated with his wife and two young children from the comfort of Tel Aviv for a promise of potentially an interesting career. At the age of 35, Armon became the youngest city engineer in all of Israel. He was responsible for planning housing and infrastructure in the region. Just a few months into his new position, the country was confronted with a sudden immigration wave of Soviet Jews, causing a severe housing shortage. Eli was leading the designing and building of 10,000 dwelling units in Be'er Sheva, resulting in a rapid growth of the city.

In 1992, Armon left his position as the city engineer but remained in Be'er Sheva to open his own practice – Armon Architects and Town Planners. He currently maintains 22 employees and is overseeing the design and construction of about 50 projects. Over the last 27 years, the architect has realized close to 100 buildings, including museums, culture and civil centers, schools, train stations, and a synagogue for the Israeli Defense Forces' Officer's Academy (it is considered the West point of the IDF). All buildings are in Israel. Eli Armon's book If Architecture Is a Language, then a Building Is a Story was published in 2018 and his solo exhibition will open next May as part of the 17th Venice Architecture Biennale. The following interview is a condensed version of our multi-hour conversation over Skype between New York and Be'er Sheva.

Architect Eli Armon, a 7th Dan master in Dennis survival Jiu-Jitsu method.

Vladimir Belogolovsky: You said that ever since you can remember you were a nomad. Could you talk about that?

Eli Armon: My given name is Eliezer, the name of Abraham's servant who was the ultimate nomad, the father of all nomads. I believe that I was given this name for a reason. Being a nomad is how I see myself in retrospect – I studied engineering, martial arts, I tried to have a career in the army, I contemplated a thought of becoming a mathematician, and then I became an architect. How am I not a nomad? I always questioned what I did. I was never satisfied. I wanted to try different fields. My philosophy is about the circle of life. I am always moving. What makes a nomad fundamentally different is that he can't remain in one place. He has to move. If you ask a nomad where he will be tomorrow, he will not give you an answer. I was born in the northern part of Tel Aviv, a very posh neighborhood. Anyone who lives there would never even think of moving to another place. But I left the comfort of city life to live in the desert. I felt a sense of mission, and I was fully supported by my beautiful wife and two small children who came along. Sure, we were not the pioneers. Still, what we did was pioneering. Looking back, I can tell you that I am very proud and happy for what we did.

VB: What did you gain by parting with city life? What did you find in the desert?

EA: The advantage of being in the periphery is that here architects have a chance to build from scratch. Emptiness means potential. It is in the emptiness that one can build the future that one can imagine. Almost all my projects are ground up buildings. They are standing without any abstractions in all their glory, seen by all.

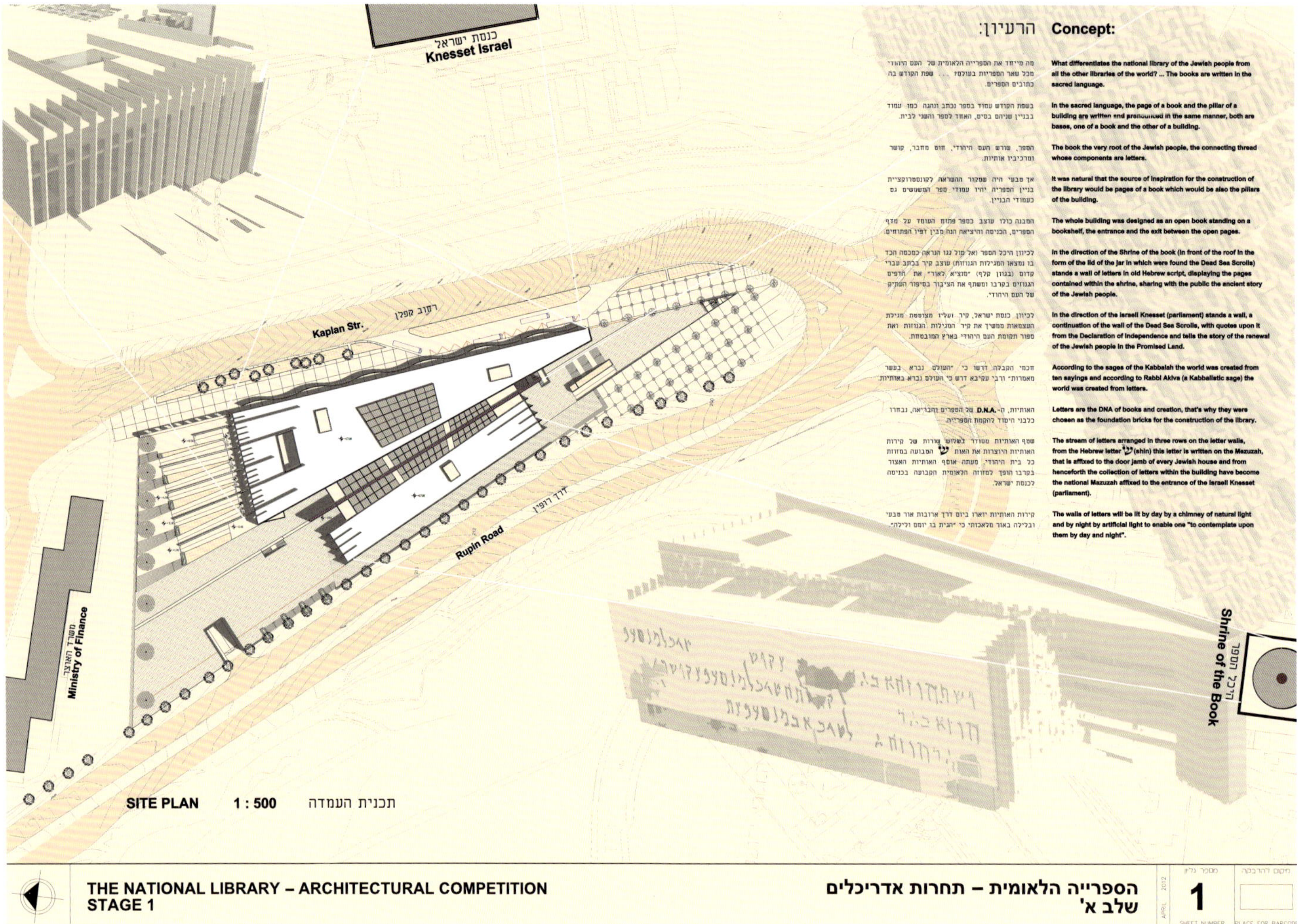

It is a divine feeling when you can leave the first mark on the ground. You put your seed in the ground, so to speak. Metaphorically speaking, you have to give your building water, light, direction, and plant it in a safe way, in harmony either with open space or other buildings. I can say that I have left an impact on the landscape. I see my buildings like beacons of light. When I wander through the dark nights in the Negev, I connect all these beacons; they are a sort of Hanukkah menorah lights for me.

On the other hand, so many buildings in Tel Aviv present themselves with an attitude. They try to prove something. I am a martial artist, not a body builder, and I am not competing in a beauty pageant. My buildings are about concentration, not showing off their muscles. I aim to win. I don't like buildings that put all their virtues on display like pretty vases and statues in a window display. There is something fragile about urban architecture, pretty but flimsy. My buildings are strong and grounded. They are rooted in the ground, rooted in the landscape. I study Kabbalah, which is about finding the roots of everything in life. I also study martial arts. To be an effective fighter you have to find your roots and power. That's what I found in the desert – my roots and power.

VB: You said that an architect is someone who makes order and harmony in the world of shapes. You said that architecture is about finding a balance between addressing function, contents, ideas, and expressing them all in three dimensions to do justice with all. What would you add about your architecture?

EA: Every project is a search for a new way. Every building is a new voyage. Every building is a new fight, of course! We are fighting all the time. And I know how to fight, believe me. [Laughs.] Sometimes, the Mayor wants this, and I want that; how can we agree? When you pick up a pen you can only succeed if you find the direct connection between the hand, heart, and soul. That's the moment when the building begins, not when you draw something random on a computer screen. What is architecture? What is creativity? Creativity comes from divine source. No one will tell you what it is. To me creativity starts when you take clay into your hand. The fingers represent restrictions – there are so many – gravity, budget, material limitations, regulations, municipalities, and so on. The clay is the architect's creativity. Then you squeeze it really hard. What you then put on the table is architecture. A good architect is all about finding a wise compromise with both inner and outer forces. Architecture is the art of finding harmony between political, economic, social, environmental, creative forces and express them in three dimensions, putting the architect's heart, faith and soul deep within. If architecture is a language, a building is a story. In other words, each building is a book. First, I write a story, then I build a building. There is no good building without a story. There is no architecture without a soul. When I say compromise, I don't mean compromising the main story. You can tell your story in 100 different ways, but the main storyline must remain intact. It cannot be compromised. I am writing my stories with my buildings. I hope my buildings can inspire people, just like books.

VB: The Book of Creation describes God's creation of the world through the manipulation of the Hebrew alphabet and ten numbers. You express your buildings through letters and stories. Why do you conceive your buildings as stories? Is the purpose to educate about history and religion?

EA: Of course, letters make up stories. With letters you build communication, you build dreams. One of my competition projects for the National Library of Israel in Jerusalem is based on this very concept – letters descending from the sky. Letters and stories have tremendous power. I envision a city as a giant library – streets as shelves and books as buildings. And if buildings are books, then the architects are writers. In Hebrew, there is a double meaning to some words. For example, the word page in Hebrew is the same as the pillar. This wordplay is a real inspiration for my architecture. In my library project, I manifested the building's pillars in a form of pages with Hebrew letters, literally.

VB: Could you talk about the origin of this concept – planning your buildings like stories? What triggered your interest in conceiving your buildings this way?

EA: When people look at any design, they have to realize that they are looking at a result, not the process. Where do the ideas come from? To me ideas come like a lightning. You cannot expect it. It can happen any time. This is how it was from the very beginning. When it comes it comes, at the time that it should come. I put real stories in real buildings. Every one of my buildings has a central space where I put all my energy, all my strength, all my creativity. I call this space a knockout. Again, I am a martial artist. My goal is the knockout. I am always looking for Chi, the internal energy of life, the spirit of each building.

VB: One of the articles about your work claims that you create beautiful buildings that are distinctly Jewish. How important is that for you – to express Jewish identity in your architecture?

EA: It is not my intention. I was born here, and this is who I am. I was chosen to live here, to build in the desert. If I were born in New York, it would be completely different. There are urban type people and there are rural type people. Urban type people are those who wear shoes and walk over concrete and asphalt. The rural type people wear no shoes and walk on sand and soil. But essentially, we are all the same. I work like a chef. I use all kinds of materials in the process of creating my architecture. What I know for sure is that to build a good building or to prepare a good meal you must add the most important ingredient, spices, which is my love for people.

Sculpture LXX-M-1, by Serbian artist Dušan Džamonja.

VB: Do you think architecture is art?

EA: Of course, it is! I believe that only when a building becomes art, architecture is born. Without art there is no architecture, just forms and facades. The ultimate dream of an architect is when architecture and art become one. That's the goal. When I finished my synagogue one of my employees showed me a picture of the flame-like sculpture by Serbian artist Dušan Džamonja. His sculpture, LXX-M-1 evokes my design for the synagogue. I have never heard of this artist before and he has never herd of me either, but somehow the architect's and sculptor's creations found each other in a conversation of their own. I find that fascinating and there is no explanation for it. Words can only do damage here. I prefer not to offer any explanation. I like when buildings and sculptures find each other. Imagine if all buildings were sculptures! A city would look like an art museum. What is it that a city wants to be? I think cities want to be art museums. Imagine, cities with buildings as sculptures; how special that would be! Every building should have a story; that's what makes architecture art. Architects are artists, of course!

VB: How did you receive the commission to design the Synagogue at the Bahad 1 military training base in the south of Israel?

EA: I was contacted by the commander of the Israeli Defense Forces' Officer's Academy, which is the top in the country because the Ministry of Defense wanted the synagogue to be designed by a local architect. When I received the commission in 2004, it took me two days to come up with the initial sketch. I didn't sleep all night. The idea came like a lightning; in the middle of the night I made my sketch, and it felt right. I didn't make any changes and it was built just like my first sketch. Sometimes you make hundreds of sketches, sometimes one sketch is all you need. Ideas come subconsciously. You can't put your finger on the source of the inspiration. Creative forces are invisible. What I can tell you is that this 280-square-meter building makes me prouder than if I won an international competition to design the tallest building in New York City! [Laughs.]

VB: This synagogue's design is based on a strong metaphor, the biblical story of the burning bush. Could you talk about that and also address the importance of metaphors in your work? There is a seed in the Ministry of Agriculture in Gilat, infinity in the Senior Citizen and Kindergarten Center in Meitar,

Moses and the Burning Bush.

blades in Lehavim-Rahat Railway Station, Abraham's well in the Tourist Center and the crack in Yad Sara, both in Be'er Sheva.

EA: I put a metaphor in the center of all my buildings. The seed, infinity, blades, Abraham's well, the crack, burning bush, all these metaphors bring meaning to my buildings. For example, the Lehavim-Rahat Railway Station is situated in Lehavim. In Hebrew, the name of this town means Blades. That's what I took as the basis for the project. A blade is all about movement. I used a whole field of enlarged blades to design the station's roof. The driving inspiration for the synagogue was the image of the burning bush because Moses received his mission in front of the burning bush.

VB: Why did you represent the burning bush as a volume, as an enclosed space for soldiers to pray in the midst of it, as opposed to depicting its image on the building's facade?

EA: What makes the uniqueness of the burning bush is that you see the flame and you enter the flame. The sentence, "The bush burned with fire, but the bush was not consumed," has served as the inspiration for designing the structure with flames. So, I wrapped the hall of prayer with 24 concrete flames – six on each of the square's four sides. Imagine, you are inside, and you are surrounded by the flames like the campfires. I think praying surrounded by the campfires is the best image you can give to soldiers before the battle. It is about preparing the soldiers for the ultimate courage, for them to fulfill their mission.

The copper main entrance door "burns" in the setting sun (above). The renowned designer, Igal Gabay, has created a series of posters inspired by Eliezer Armon's buildings. This piece relates to The Burning Bush Synagogue of Bahad 1 (right).

I used very few materials in this project. Concrete for undulating panels that make up the flame. Stone for the floor, which comes from the quarry just three kilometers away. Glass with no aluminum frames. And copper for the central entry door. It faces west and appears to be on fire every time the sun hits it at the sunset. We literally invented all the details and connections, using raw materials in the most basic ways. Nothing is perfect in this building because the war is tough. The war is brutal; it is ruthless. It is not about the building, it is about praying. We took the materials, we took the sun, and we made the building.

VB: This synagogue is tiny, and it has only one central space raised one level above the classrooms and facilities on the ground floor.

EA: Exactly. Every structure I design has one central space, which contains the entire story. This is where I assemble the entire power, like a martial artist who focuses all the strengths of his body into a single spot. In other projects, you have many spaces and many chances but here there was only one chance, it had to be a knockout project. It is either a knockout or nothing. We raised the praying hall to detach soldiers from the ground to connect them with spiritual feeling.

VB: Photos show that soldiers come here to pray with their rifles.

EA: It is a story within a story. In the Bible, Gideon, a military leader, judge, and prophet, would only appoint those soldiers to fight who never part with their weapons. That's why in the synagogue the officers hold their rifles as they pray. Every officer during their training at this camp must go through the synagogue. This building plays an important role in educating people.

VB: Have you discovered something new by completing this project? Was there a particular surprise during either the design or construction process?

EA: Well, we knew from the start that we were embarking on a non-conventional project and that we would be facing many problems. For example, when we were installing the flame panels, the very first one broke and we had to come up with a different installation technique. When something is done for the first time a solution needs to be found. Every day we were facing new challenges. We were on a mission; it was not just another project. This is what every architect needs to be aspired to – being the first. If you simply want to complete a project that's one thing, but if you want to say something with your work, if you want people to experience and learn something new then you have to be original every time. This may not sound humble, but it is. As an architect, I want my buildings to give something back. It is not about taking but giving.

וַיַּרְא
וְהִנֵּה
הַסְּנֶה
בֹּעֵר
בָּאֵשׁ
וְהַסְּנֶה
אֵינֶנּוּ
אֻכָּל
Igal Gabay | Graphic Design Studio

EPILOGUE

BY BRIGADIER GENERAL GAL HIRSCH

I had the honor and privilege of being the commandant of Israel Defense Forces' Officer's Academy in 2003-2005.

This base is unique and one cannot consider it as a regular military unit. It is special and significantly important, and since it has trained new leaders for the Israel Defense Forces since it was established, it is well-known among Israeli citizens as a national strategic institute, and many Israeli teenagers dream to be among its graduates.

Along with its independence, Israel had to fight for its security and an important brick in the Israeli security wall is the quality of its leaders, commanders and officers.

The credo of an Israeli officer is never "go ahead" or "let's go"; an Israeli officer will always command "follow me" and according to the Biblical words of Judge Gideon who said "watch me and do likewise," the Israeli officer will be always the first to go, to risk himself and storm the enemy under fire. This is also one of the reasons for the huge number of casualties among Israeli officers: they are leading the way all the way and it doesn't matter what rank they have – you may find a captain fighting alongside a colonel or even General in the battlefield, because leading by personal example is one of the crucial lessons of a cadet in the Officer's Academy.

During my tenure as commandant, I had to lead the school through many challenges and reforms. We had to update our curriculum and adapt the training program to many new changes in battlefields such as asymmetric warfare, counter-terrorism and counter insurgency, and so on and so forth. However, we also had to take care and deal with other special challenges regarding the Israeli society and its structure.

I decided to cancel the separation between female and male in officers' training and by that to close the female training base and integrate the cadets from both genders. It created a big public dispute in Israeli society but I insisted that there would not be any more separated schools, only rooms and bathrooms would be separated.

Another decision that created public dispute was my decision to put Judaism and Jewish legacy as a part of the syllabus and curriculum. I was and always will be sure that an Israeli leader must know our legacy and history and know what he is fighting for and exactly what he is defending.

An immediate result of these two decisions was a third one: to build a new synagogue for the training base, one that was not only a building but to symbolize our beliefs, to integrate ca-

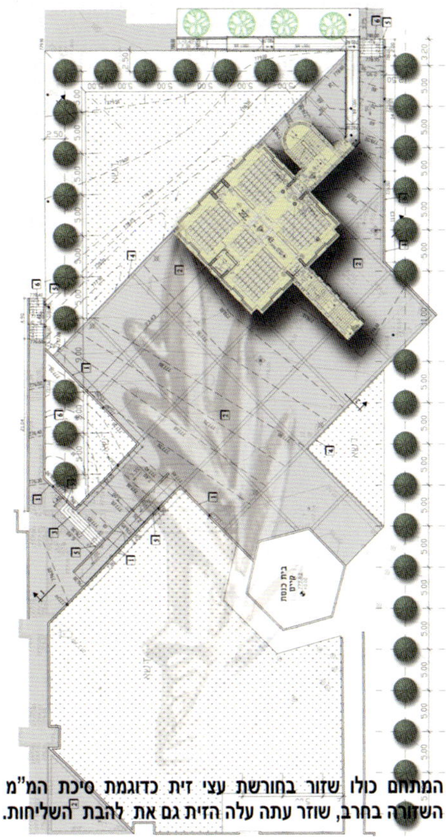

A presentation illustration of the synagogue and its surrounding from above.

BRIGADIER GENERAL GAL HIRSCH (Ret.) is one of the most experienced in the IDF (Israel Defense Forces) in the areas of Counter Terrorism, Counter Insurgency and Guerilla Warfare. He spearheaded Israel's fight against terror for 35 years in all fronts as a commander of several elite units and as a field officer. He is a decorated soldier whose overt activities are well known and highly acclaimed in the security circles in Israel and its allies. Hirsch is an expert in Strategy, Leadership and Innovation, in the last decade. He manages several R&D (research and development) and cutting edge technology projects.

dets from both genders in praying and preserving the Jewish legacy and habits. I circulated this idea among my staff and close team members. The famous officer training school's NCO (Non-commissioned-officer) Itzhak Taito who has served there for decades suggested that we meet Eliezer Armon. "He is special," he smiled, "you will find the right person for your crazy ideas." The meetings with Eliezer were stormy indeed; we have immediately found many topics to argue about. His imagination reminded me of the way I worked for many years with my special forces – where there are no limits for imagination and where creativity is a necessity.

When his mind crushed into mine we could position ourselves as a satellite, looking for new dimensions and trying to look for metaphors and act accordingly. For Eliezer every project is a story, each part of the building is a chapter – words and letters.

The turbulence our brainstorming created found its way to the architect's table and into successful design and planning. This is why Eliezer is until today a part of my planning team for special missions.

As mentioned before, a lot of the Israel Defense Forces' inspiration and spirit comes from the Bible, and it was clear we will take the burning bush as an important symbol and that combination between the sword (rifle) and the book (Bible) will remain an integral part of a cadet's life, even while praying.

Along the years, I served as a field officer: platoon leader, company commander, unite commander, battalion commander, brigade commander, division commander and the commander of the Israeli special forces.

Our combat service is combined with technologies, war machines and methodologies, but as an experienced commander, I know for sure that with no spirit, morals, values and symbols we will not win the wars.

With no biblical roots and spirit, we will not be able to defend the state of Israel and the Jewish people – this is why The Burning Bush Synagogue is so special, an important and unique project in the Israel Defense Forces' history.

APPENDIX

BIOGRAPHY

Architect Eliezer Armon, has served as chief city engineer for the Emanuel Regional Council and for the City of Beer Sheva. Since 1993, he has been at the helm of Armon Architects and Town Planners, Ltd., which incorporates the full range of architectural planning, starting with furniture design, to interior design, to structure planning, up to and encompassing urban planning.

His multidisciplinary personality transcends conventional professional perceptions, viewing architectural planning as the incarnation of ideas, existential insights and life cycles that materialize as one seamless, multifaceted creation.

His work is the craft of the inquisitive researcher, deriving from Jewish holy and literary sources, the Hebrew language, Jewish tradition, Kabbalah, the Land of Israel and its landscapes, world cultures, and the universality of the martial arts with all their meaning.

His works are fueled by endless propelling toward the root and origin of the creation. His perspective is interwoven with the cognitive correlation between military leadership and architecture. The saying "architect of victory" is not just by chance.

Armon Architects and Town Planners operates on a wide national spread, simultaneously planning and managing dozens of projects from Ma'alot-Tarshiha in the north to Eilat in the south.

Armon, born in Tel Aviv, pupil of Ken Borochov Working and Studying Youth Movement, Practical Electronics Engineer, graduate of ORT Yad Singalovski Vocational School, Lieutenant Colonel (reserves), graduate of the Faculty of Architecture and Town Planning at the Technion Israel Institute of Technology, holding a 7th Dan Belt of the Dennis Survival jiu-jitsu method.

PROJECT CREDITS

Location
Mitzpe Ramon, Israel

Client
The Construction and Engineering Branch of the Israeli Ministry of Defence

Project
2007

Completion
2009

Area
365 square meters, main building and 57 square meters, outdoor stairs

Budget
5 million Israeli Shekel (approximately 1,5 million USD)

Architect
Armon Architects and Town Planners Ltd

Design Team
Eliezer Armon, principal in charge; Sabadosh Benjamin, Igal Rubchinsky, Idit Shelach and Marina Gurianov

Interior Design
Armon Architects and Town Planners Ltd

Landscape Architect
Gad Barkay

Photography
Uriel Messa, Sabadosh Benjamin, Eliezer Armon and Oscar Riera Ojeda

Poster Graphic Series
Igal Gabay | Graphic Design Studio
Images on pages 177 and 237

CONSTRUCTION

General Contractor
Lesico Group

Project Manager
Ministry of Defence, Negev District
Igor Starosta

Ground Work
Engineer Zelio Diamandi

Land Surveying
Erez Surveying Ltd., Be'er Sheva

Structural Engineering
Civil Engineers Moshe Lavie - Refael Badt

Mechanical, and Electrical Engineering
Barabash Orlan

Heating and Cooling
Itshak Barrabi Engineering

Plumbing System
Gal Engineering

Concrete Flames
Wolfman Industries Ltd., Ashkelon

Glazing
Amar Glass Netivot LTD

Metal Work
Shushan Gates

Doors
Delouya Design, Beersheba

Acoustics
Top Consulting and Engineering Ltd.

Lighting Design
Barabash Orlan

CONSTRIBUTORS

The Synagogue was built with the generous support and assitance of the Ruderman Family Foundation.

The Synagogue's furniture was executed with the generous donation of the LIBI France, and several of their members including the following families and or individuals: Malka, Sultan, Toledano, Hela Tweena, Tordjman, Gahnasia, Tzarevcan, Mr. Yaacov Rhoum, Edgar Adda, Herve Adda, David Abergel, Héléne Ohana, Meyer Ohana, Lilu Ohana, and Gilbert Haddad.

PHOTOGRAPHY CAPTIONS

The southern view at twilight as the Synagogue is lit up.
Photograph by Uriel Messa.

A view of the synagogue from the gathering plaza at Bahad 1 Military Academy where the rank awarding ceremonies are commonly held.
Photograph by Uriel Messa.

Existing conditions prior to the erection of the building.
View from southwest.
Photograph by Eliezer Armon.

Existing conditions prior to the erection of the building.
View from west.
Photograph by Eliezer Armon.

Synagogue's base foundation.
Photograph by Eliezer Armon.

The old base Synagogue designed by Alfred Neumann and Zvi Hecker.
Photograph by Eliezer Armon.

Experimental castings of the concrete are inspected by the Chief Inspector of the Ministry of Defense – Igor Starosa.
Photograph by Eliezer Armon.

Wood scaffolding erected to aid the construction of concrete walls.
Photograph by Eliezer Armon.

View of the upper corner with the glass anchored to the concrete with metal connections.
Photograph by Sabadosh Benjamin.

The building's facade shows the staircase leading up to the Prayer Hall.
Photograph by Uriel Messa.

Existing conditions prior to the erection of the building.
View from northeast.
Photograph by Eliezer Armon.

Preliminary ground works and foundations construction.
Photograph by Eliezer Armon.

Architect Eliezer Armon supervising the synagogue's foundations construction.
Photograph by Sabadosh Benjamin.

Completion of the first base wall.
Photograph by Eliezer Armon.

Concrete work completed of the base perimeter walls.
Photograph by Eliezer Armon.

Wood scaffolding erected to aid the construction of concrete walls.
Photograph by Eliezer Armon.

Construction of the skeleton structure.
Photograph by Eliezer Armon.

The skeleton structure base.
Photograph by Eliezer Armon.

Ground floor of the skeleton structure.
Photograph by Eliezer Armon.

Construction of the skeleton structure, view from the main staircase.
Photograph by Eliezer Armon.

The reinforced steel mesh flame structure prior to concrete pouring.
Photograph by Eliezer Armon.

The reinforced steel mesh flame structure prior to concrete pouring.
Photograph by Eliezer Armon.

Bending of the steel rods is done using a stencil that is fixed to the floor.
Photograph by Eliezer Armon.

The reinforced steel mesh flame structure prior to concrete pouring.
Photograph by Eliezer Armon.

Construction of the skeleton structure.
Photograph by Eliezer Armon.

View of the skeleton structure as seen from the staircase leading up to the Women's section.
Photograph by Eliezer Armon.

Ground floor of the skeleton structure.
Photograph by Eliezer Armon.

View of the skeleton structure as seen from the staircase leading up to the Women's section.
Photograph by Eliezer Armon.

The reinforced steel mesh flame structure prior to concrete pouring.
Photograph by Eliezer Armon.

Bending of the steel rods is done using a stencil that is fixed to the floor.
Photograph by Eliezer Armon.

The plates joined to the floor just before being covered with concrete.
Photograph by Eliezer Armon.

Armon supervising the construction of the concrete flames.
Photograph by Sabadosh Benjamin.

The planning and supervision team of the Ministry of Defense and the planners, headed by colonel and commander of Bahad 1 at the time - Aharon Haliva, are touring the Wolfman Industries factory where the concrete flames are poured. From right to left: Aharon Haliva, Eli Armon, Viki lichstien, Daniel Rode, Igor Starosa. Photograph by Sabadosh Benjamin.

Details of the steel mesh.
Photograph by Eliezer Armon.

Details of the steel mesh.
Photograph by Eliezer Armon.

Details of the steel mesh.
Photograph by Eliezer Armon.

Details of the steel mesh.
Photograph by Eliezer Armon.

Checking the binding of the steel mesh to the mold before it's closed.
Photograph by Eliezer Armon.

Checking the binding of the steel mesh to the mold before it's closed.
Photograph by Sabadosh Benjamin.

Checking the binding of the steel mesh to the mold before it's closed.
Photograph by Eliezer Armon.

Pre-construction of the steel flame being assembled at the factory site (Wolfman Industries).
Photograph by Sabadosh Benjamin.

Architect Eliezer Armon supervising the construction of the concrete flames.
Photograph by Sabadosh Benjamin.

Architect Eliezer Armon supervising the construction of the concrete flames.
Photograph by Sabadosh Benjamin.

Achitect Eliezer Armon and the commander of Bahad 1 at the time - Aharon Haliva, supervising the construction of the concrete flames.
Photograph by Sabadosh Benjamin.

The curing process.
Photograph by Eliezer Armon.

The curing process.
Photograph by Eliezer Armon.

The curing process.
Photograph by Eliezer Armon.

Closing the flame mold before pouring concrete.
Photograph by Eliezer Armon.

Pouring the concrete.
Photograph by Eliezer Armon.

Architect Eliezer Armon and the commander of BAHAD 1 at the time - Aharon Haliva, supervising the construction of the concrete flames.
Photograph by Sabadosh Benjamin.

The concrete flames are ready for transportation.
Photograph by Eliezer Armon.

The concrete flames are ready for transportation.
Photograph by Eliezer Armon.

The concrete flames are ready for transportation.
Photograph by Eliezer Armon.

The concrete flames are ready for transportation.
Photograph by Eliezer Armon.

At the factory site (Wolfman Industries).
Photograph by Eliezer Armon.

The destined base of the concrete flames.
Photograph by Eliezer Armon.

Inspection from above before closing the mold.
Photograph by Eliezer Armon.

The concrete flames are ready for transportation.
Photograph by Eliezer Armon.

Architect Eliezer Armon and the commander of BAHAD 1 at the time - Aharon Haliva, supervising the construction of the concrete flames.
Photograph by Sabadosh Benjamin.

The concrete flames are ready for transportation.
Photograph by Eliezer Armon.

The edge of the concrete flame.
Photograph by Eliezer Armon.

Inner view of the skeleton structure.
Photograph by Eliezer Armon.

The skeleton structure waiting to be covered by the concrete flames.
Photograph by Eliezer Armon.

The skeleton structure waiting to be covered by the concrete flames.
Photograph by Eliezer Armon.

View of the skeleton structure as seen from the staircase leading up to the Women's section. Photograph by Eliezer Armon.

The Women's section. Photograph by Eliezer Armon.

View on the base from inside the skeleton structure. Photograph by Eliezer Armon.

Ground floor. Photograph by Eliezer Armon.

View of the skeleton structure as seen from the staircase leading up to the Women's section. Photograph by Eliezer Armon.

The concrete flames arrive at the site. Photograph by Eliezer Armon.

The concrete flames arrive at the site. Photograph by Eliezer Armon.

View of the skeleton structure as seen from the staircase leading up to the Women's section. Photograph by Eliezer Armon.

The roofless skeleton structure. Photograph by Eliezer Armon.

Base of the staircase. Photograph by Eliezer Armon.

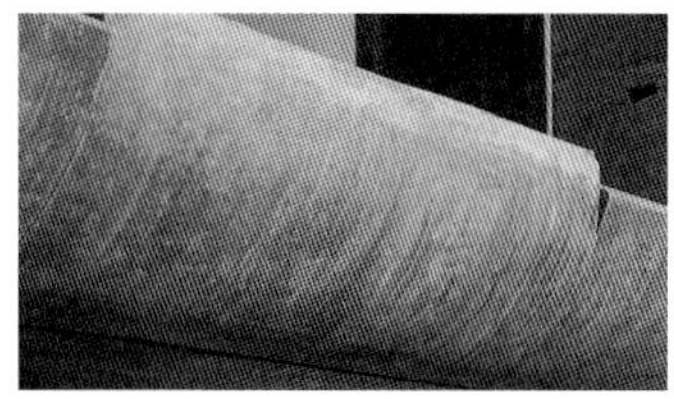
Base of the skeleton structure. Photograph by Eliezer Armon.

Stairs leading to Women's section. Photograph by Eliezer Armon.

The edge of the floor is geometrically aligned for receiving the flame element. Photograph by Eliezer Armon.

Installation of the concrete flames. Photograph by Eliezer Armon.

Installation of the concrete flames. Photograph by Eliezer Armon.

Installation of the concrete flames. Photograph by Eliezer Armon.

Installation of the concrete flames.
Photograph by Eliezer Armon.

Installation of the concrete flames.
Photograph by Eliezer Armon.

Installation of the concrete flames.
Photograph by Eliezer Armon.

A moment of crisis. The concrete foot cracks.
Photograph by Eliezer Armon.

Installation of the concrete flames.
Photograph by Eliezer Armon.

Installation of the concrete flames.
Photograph by Eliezer Armon.

Installation of the concrete flames.
Photograph by Eliezer Armon.

Installation of the concrete flames.
Photograph by Eliezer Armon.

Installation of the concrete flames.
Photograph by Eliezer Armon.

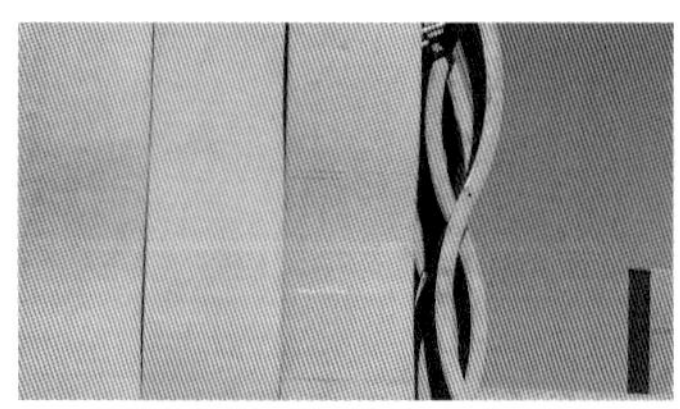

Installation of the concrete flames.
Photograph by Eliezer Armon.

The edge of the floor is geometrically aligned for receiving the flame element.
Photograph by Eliezer Armon.

A view on the platform leading to the woman section.
Photograph by Eliezer Armon.

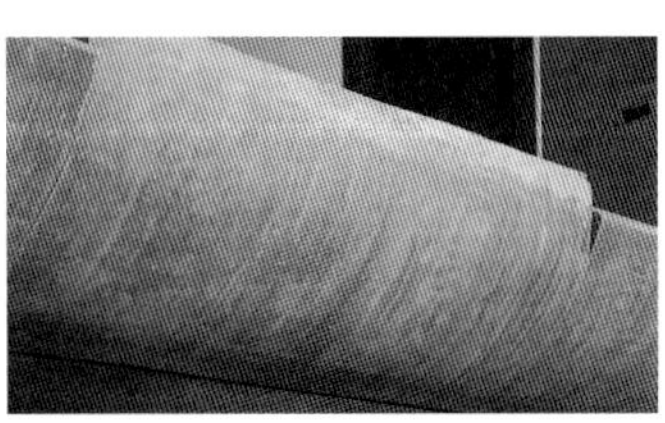

Base of the skeleton structure.
Photograph by Eliezer Armon.

Attaching the flame element to the roof.
Photograph by Eliezer Armon.

Attaching the flame element to the roof.
Photograph by Eliezer Armon.

Attaching the flame element to the roof.
Photograph by Eliezer Armon.

Attaching the flame element
to the roof.
Photograph by Eliezer Armon.

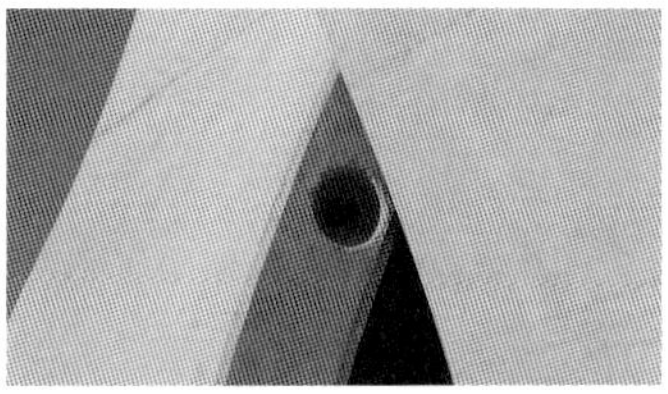
A view of the flames from the inside
after installation.
Photograph by Eliezer Armon.

The front view of the synagogue
after the flames installation.
Photograph by Eliezer Armon.

Main entrance after the
flames installation.
Photograph by Eliezer Armon.

The front view of the synagogue
after the flames installation.
Photograph by Eliezer Armon.

Inside look of the woman section
after the flames installation.
Photograph by Eliezer Armon.

Base of the flames.
Photograph by Eliezer Armon.

A view from inside of the aligned
concrete flames.
Photograph by Eliezer Armon.

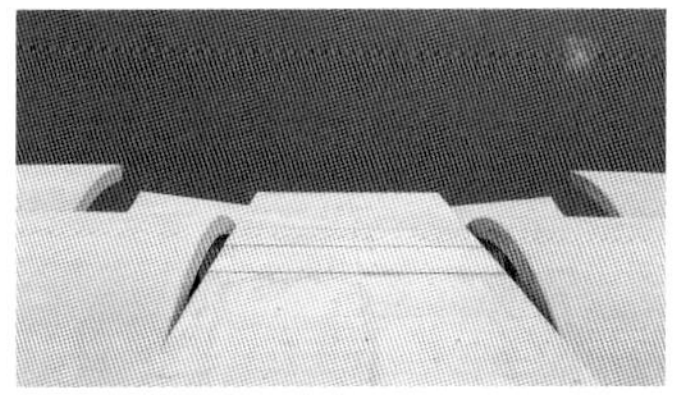
Attaching the flame element
to the roof.
Photograph by Eliezer Armon.

A view of the flames from the inside
after installation.
Photograph by Eliezer Armon.

The front view of the synagogue after
the flames installation.
Photograph by Eliezer Armon.

The front view of the synagogue
after the flames installation.
Photograph by Eliezer Armon.

Base of the flames.
Photograph by Eliezer Armon.

Base of the flames.
Photograph by Eliezer Armon.

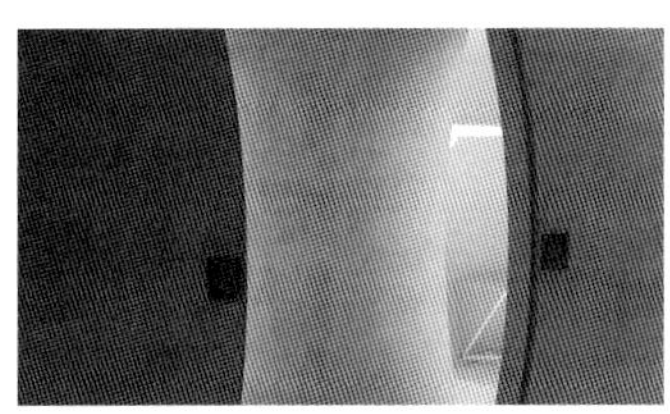
A view from inside of the aligned
concrete flames.
Photograph by Eliezer Armon.

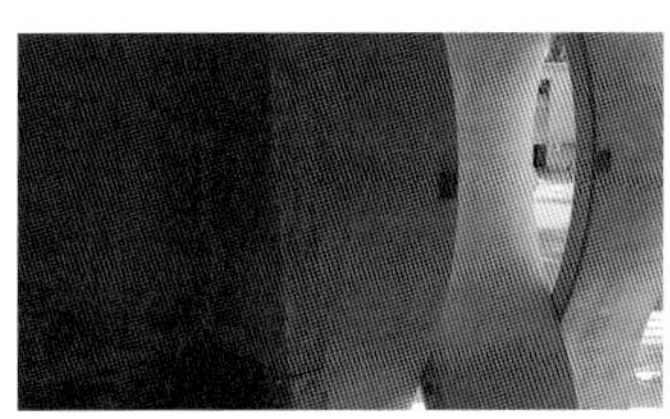
A view from inside of the aligned
concrete flames.
Photograph by Eliezer Armon.

Close up detail of concrete flames.
Photograph by Eliezer Armon.

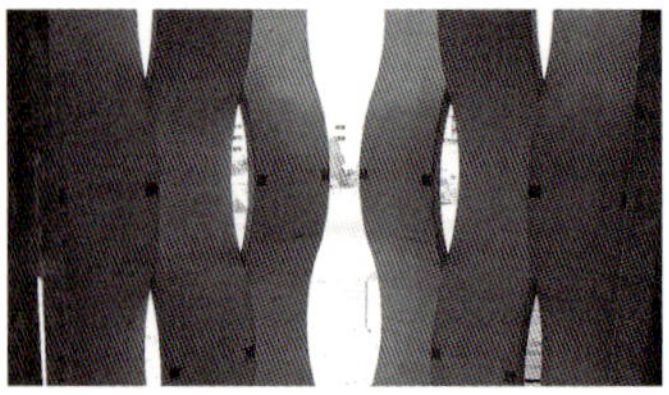

A view of the flames from the inside after installation.
Photograph by Eliezer Armon.

Interior view of southwest corner with all flames in postion prior to glass installation.
Photograph by Eliezer Armon.

Builder holding casting mold used for window frame installation.
Photograph by Eliezer Armon.

Builder holding metal window frames prior to the installation.
Photograph by Eliezer Armon.

Prayer platfrom prior to its construction.
Photograph by Eliezer Armon.

Close up detail of the connection between two concrete flame edges.
Photograph by Eliezer Armon.

Bahad 1 academy parade ceremony with distant synagogue view.
Photograph by Uriel Messa.

Ceiling and flames connection showing cenital light conditions.
Photograph by Eliezer Armon.

Sensual view of curving flames.
Photograph by Eliezer Armon.

A view from the secondary entrance to the prayer hall prior to closing the flames.
Photograph by Eliezer Armon.

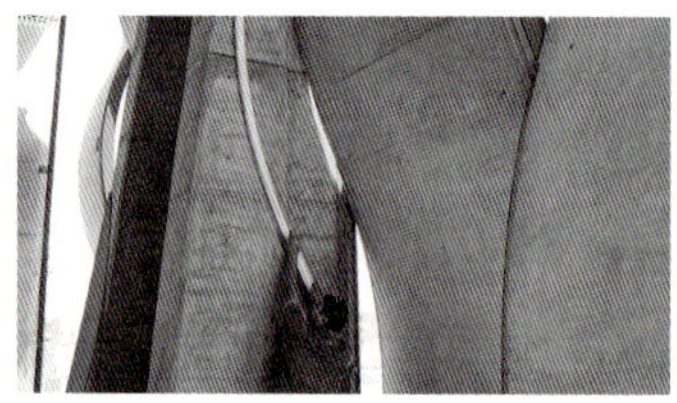

Builder holding metal window frame prior to installation.
Photograph by Eliezer Armon.

Stainless steel glass supports.
Photograph by Eliezer Armon.

Stainless steel glass supports and their connection to the concrete flames.
Photograph by Eliezer Armon.

Last stages of interior finishes.
Photograph by Eliezer Armon.

Distant view of the synagogue with other academy buildings beyond.
Photograph by Uriel Messa.

Distant view of the synagogue with other academy buildings beyond.
Photograph by Uriel Messa.

The epitaph which inspired the construction of the building is affixed on the main entrance stair base wall.
Photograph by Uriel Messa.

Southwest general view.
Photograph by Uriel Messa.

Main entry stair stainless steel handrail detail.
Photograph by Uriel Messa.

Chief NCO Taito, who has led the IDF's Officer's Academy since its establishment, climbs up the stairs. He's also the man that initially introduced architect Eli Armon and Gal Hirsh, BAHAD 1 commander at the time.
Photograph by Sabadosh Benjamin.

The entrance as seen from the main door.
Photograph by Oscar Riera Ojeda.

Memorial plaque commemorating the Ruderman family who donated the majority of the budget needed for the construction of the building.
Photograph by Oscar Riera Ojeda.

Menorah symbol detail view below Women's section mezzanine floor.
Photograph by Uriel Messa.

The old base synagogue designed by Alfred Neumann and Zvi Hecker.
Photograph by Uriel Messa.

West facade view.
Photograph by Uriel Messa.

Principal stair leading to the main synagogue's entry.
Photograph by Eliezer Armon.

View of the main entrance. Standing on the stairs is Chief NCO Taito.
Photograph by Sabadosh Benjamin.

South elevation view with stairs leading to the main synagogue's entrance.
Photograph by Sabadosh Benjamin.

Straight view of prayers hall from main entry.
Photograph by Uriel Messa.

General view of the prayers hall from the main entry.
Photograph by Uriel Messa.

A view of the prayer hall from the main entry towards the secondary entry with Menorah symbol floating from the Women's section ceiling.
Photograph by Uriel Messa.

A view from the prayer hall towards the secondary entry and the Women's section.
Photograph by Uriel Messa.

A view from the prayer hall towards the secondary entry and the Women's section.
Photograph by Uriel Messa.

A view of the prayer platform (Bimah).
Photograph by Uriel Messa.

Close up view of the prayer platform (Bimah).
Photograph by Uriel Messa.

A prayer stand imitates a weapon's barrel as inspired by the story of Gideon in the book of Judges.
Photograph by Eliezer Armon.

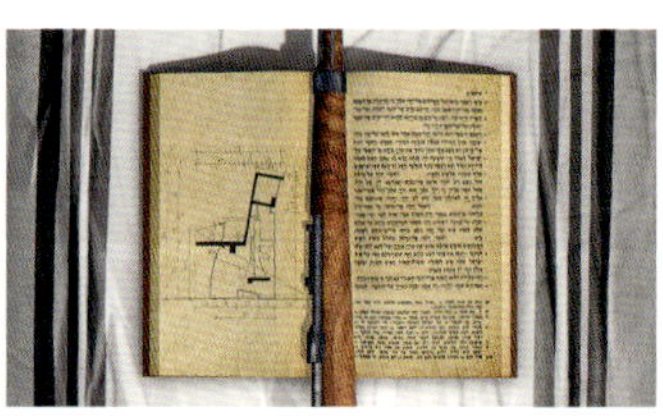

The renowned designer, Igal Gabay, has created a series of posters inspired by Eliezer Armon's buildings. This piece relates to the the praying stool in The Burning Bush Synagogue of Bahad 1.
Photograph by Eliezer Armon.

Attaching the glasswork using metal posts.
Photograph by Eliezer Armon.

View from the the back entry towards the prayer hall.
Photograph by Uriel Messa.

Secondary entry.
Photograph by Uriel Messa.

Prayer platform in front of the Holy Ark.
Photograph by Uriel Messa.

The prayer platform (Bimah) and the Holy Ark (Aron Ha'kodesh) viewed from the Women's section.
Photograph by Uriel Messa.

View towards the prayer hall and the main entrance.
Photograph by Uriel Messa.

A prayer stand imitates a weapon's barrel as inspired by the story of Gideon in the book of Judges.
Photograph by Eliezer Armon.

Concrete flames interior view.
Photograph by Eliezer Armon.

Close up detail of the attached glasswork with metal posts.
Photograph by Eliezer Armon.

The prayer platform (Bimah) and the Holy Ark (Aron Ha'kodesh) viewed from the Women's section.
Photograph by Uriel Messa.

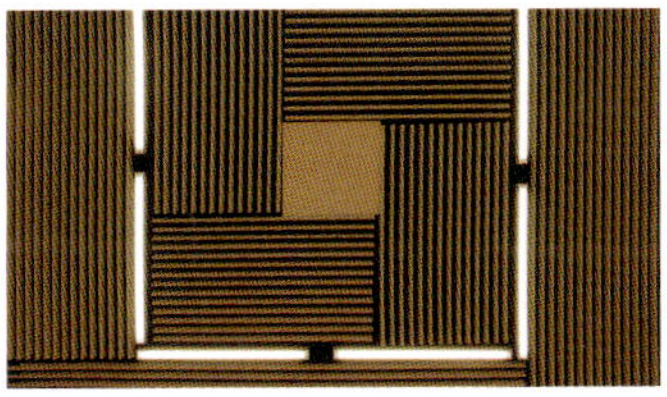

Main ceiling detail.
Photograph by Sabadosh Benjamin.

Southwest corner of main prayer hall with academy buildings beyond.
Photograph by Sabadosh Benjamin.

Main hall northwest corner from Women's section at mezzanine floor.
Photograph by Sabadosh Benjamin.

General view of Women's section at mezzanine floor.
Photograph by Oscar Riera Ojeda.

Interior view of northwest corner.
Photograph by Uriel Messa.

Interior corner view showing how glass, flames, ceiling and supports come together.
Photograph by Uriel Messa.

Corner view with desert beyond.
Photograph by Eliezer Armon.

Detail of concrete flames and stair handrail.
Photograph by Sabadosh Benjamin.

The Menorah, Israel's symbol, "floats" above the congregants' heads.
Photograph by Uriel Messa.

Northwest corner of main prayer hall with academy buildings beyond.
Photograph by Sabadosh Benjamin.

Women's section at mezzanine floor with entry/exit door.
Photograph by Oscar Riera Ojeda.

Wood detail with hidden cache for air conditioners.
Photograph by Eliezer Armon.

A view of the ceiling. The flames elements and the glasswork are joined to steel posts.
Photograph by Eliezer Armon.

A view of the ceiling. The flames elements and the glasswork are joined to steel posts.
Photograph by Uriel Messa.

Stainless steel accessories attach glass to flame elements.
Photograph by Eliezer Armon.

Corner detail showing interior ceiling lights.
Photograph by Sabadosh Benjamin.

Observing the building's corner creates a kaleidoscope effect.
Photograph by Sabadosh Benjamin.

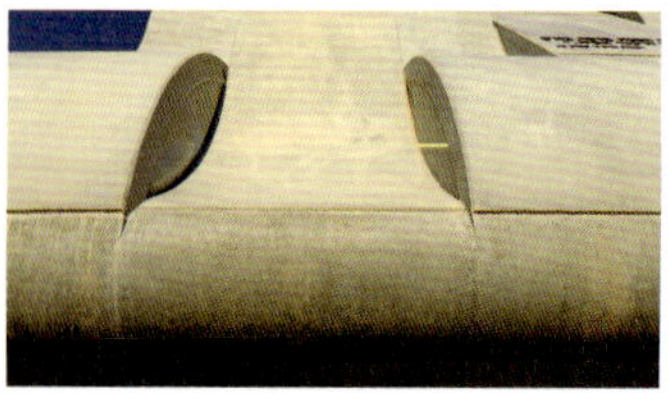

Close up round concrete detail at elevated base.
Photograph by Sabadosh Benjamin.

General eastern view.
Photograph by Sabadosh Benjamin.

Side view at base.
Photograph by Uriel Messa.

Northeastern facade at sunset.
Photograph by Uriel Messa.

Back entry doors with "burning" sunset reflection.
Photograph by Sabadosh Benjamin.

A view showing the dynamic stair design at the back entry.
Photograph by Sabadosh Benjamin.

Back entry stairs from below.
Photograph by Sabadosh Benjamin.

Southeast corner general view.
Photograph by Sabadosh Benjamin.

Window, flame and round base detail.
Photograph by Sabadosh Benjamin.

Detail of corner and stairs to back door entry.
Photograph by Uriel Messa.

Stairs to the back entry with cooper door "burning" at sunset.
Photograph by Uriel Messa.

Northwest partial view.
Photograph by Uriel Messa.

Steel handrail detail at ramp and stair.
Photograph by Sabadosh Benjamin.

East view showing entry ramp and stairs.
Photograph by Sabadosh Benjamin.

Stairs leading up to the two back entry levels.
Photograph by Sabadosh Benjamin.

Detail of curving concrete flames revealing glass sections.
Photograph by Sabadosh Benjamin.

Corner detail of concrete flames with reflected shadow.
Photograph by Sabadosh Benjamin.

Detail of concrete flame at sunset.
Photograph by Sabadosh Benjamin.

Sequence of the synagogue's changing lights conditions from late afternoon into early evening.
Photograph by Uriel Messa.

Sequence of the synagogue's changing lights conditions from late afternoon into early evening.
Photograph by Uriel Messa.

Sequence of the synagogue's changing lights conditions from late afternoon into early evening.
Photograph by Uriel Messa.

Sequence of the synagogue's changing lights conditions from late afternoon into early evening.
Photograph by Uriel Messa.

Synagogue at dusk.
Photograph by Sabadosh Benjamin.

Curving concrete flames.
Photograph by Sabadosh Benjamin.

Staircase bannister at back door upper floor entry.
Photograph by Sabadosh Benjamin.

Sequence of the synagogue's changing lights conditions from late afternoon into early evening.
Photograph by Uriel Messa.

Sequence of the synagogue's changing lights conditions from late afternoon into early evening.
Photograph by Uriel Messa.

Sequence of the synagogue's changing lights conditions from late afternoon into early evening.
Photograph by Uriel Messa.

Sequence of the synagogue's changing lights conditions from late afternoon into early evening.
Photograph by Uriel Messa.

Southwest corner at dusk.
Photograph by Uriel Messa.

Exterior corner detail of ground hall level.
Photograph by Uriel Messa.

Upper part of flames and round backstair entry at dusk with illuminated interior.
Photograph by Sabadosh Benjamin.

Overall evening view of prayers hall from main entry.
Photograph by Uriel Messa.

Ceiling and mezzanine view from prayers' platform towards the back entry.
Photograph by Uriel Messa.

Upper part of flames at dusk with illuminated interior.
Photograph by Sabadosh Benjamin.

A sunset view of the back entry bridge.
Photograph by Uriel Messa.

Concrete flame detail with back entry bridge handrail shadows.
Photograph by Uriel Messa.

The Menorah, Israel's symbol, "floats" above the congregants' heads.
Photograph by Uriel Messa.

General view from prayers hall from main entry.
Photograph by Uriel Messa.

Corner detail showing how concrete floor, glass and steel supports come together.
Photograph by Uriel Messa.

The back entry bridge at twilight.
Photograph by Uriel Messa.

The synagogue "burning" during the opening ceremony.
Photograph by Sabadosh Benjamin.

The copper main entry door glows at sunset.
Photograph by Uriel Messa.

"..והנה הסנה בוער באש
והסנה איננו אכל.."
(שמות פרק ג' פסוק ב')

BOOK CREDITS

Book Layout by Oscar Riera Ojeda
Copy Editing: Michael W. Phillips Jr.

OSCAR RIERA OJEDA
PUBLISHERS

ISBN 978-1-946226-40-2
Published by Oscar Riera Ojeda Publishers Limited
Printed in China

Oscar Riera Ojeda Publishers Limited
Unit 1003-04, 10/F.,
Shanghai Industrial Investment Building,
48-62 Hennessy Road, Wanchai, Hong Kong
T: +852-3920-9300

Production Offices | China
Suit 19, Shenyun Road,
Nanshan District, Shenzhen 518055
T: +1-484-502-5400

www.oropublishers.com | www.oscarrieraojeda.com
oscar@oscarrieraojeda.com